Curiosities of South Australia

2

RUSSELL SMITH

SMITH
books

The publication of CURIOSITIES OF SOUTH AUSTRALIA was supported by the South Australian Government through the State History Centre, a Division of the History Trust of South Australia.

Additional copies of books 1 and 2 in this series are available from:
>   Smithbooks
>   PO Box 17
>   Athelstone
>   South Australia 5076

Published for Smithbooks by Peacock Publications
38 Sydenham Road, Norwood, South Australia 5067
Copyright © Russell Smith 1999
First published July, 1999
National Library of Australia Card Number & ISBN 1 876087 27 7
Designed and produced by Peacock Publications, Adelaide
Printed by Peacock Publications, Adelaide

Contents

Introduction

In 'Curiosities of South Australia', the first book in this series, a story appeared entitled 'Royal Trees'. It told of some of the earlier trees planted by Royalty in South Australia, including a gum planted by Prince Alfred at Gawler in 1867. Mention was made of the disappearance, prior to the event, of the specially prepared spade and the young Prince being obliged to perform his duty with an 'ordinary' spade, which no doubt was suitably memorialised afterwards.

There is a remarkable sequel to that embarrassing happening. In 1996 the spade handle, complete with engraved silver plaque, turned up in a rubbish skip in a recycling yard in Wiltshire, England. It is unclear at this stage whether it was from the original spade or the substitute. Where the handle had been for the past 130 years and who threw it away in their rubbish remains a mystery.

The finder of the treasure, the recycling yard proprietor, rescued the handle when the fickle English sun reflected from the silver plaque as he was about to toss it with other scrap timber onto a fire. Had it been a normal overcast Wiltshire day that rare piece of South Australiana would have been lost forever.

So, through sheer chance, an alert Englishman is now the proud owner of a unique historical curio. We here in South Australia can be thankful for the fact and have yet another curious incident to wonder about.

The Adelaide Mayor Who Tippled Then Toppled

A large crowd quickly gathered in North Adelaide's Kermode Street on the steamy-hot evening of Tuesday, 10th February, 1857. They were drawn together by the entertaining antics of Adelaide's third Mayor, the unpredictable Joseph Hall. It was not a political meeting of any kind, the civic leader was simply blind-drunk and performing at his best. From his stage-like position on the overhanging verandah of Henry Staines' grocery shop, which was directly behind where St. Peter's Cathedral now stands, Hall looked down on the growing throng and gave them a performance most would remember for the rest of their lives.

He was well known for his unusual behaviour and the audience sensed the brewing of a similar episode to that which occurred some time earlier, when His Worship cavorted through the North Parklands in his nightshirt. They were to be disappointed. What happened that night became no laughing matter.

Little is known these days about Joseph Hall. He does not feature widely in recorded historical anecdotes, as do Mayor No. 1 and Mayor No. 2, James Hurtle Fisher and Thomas Wilson. He does not even rate a portrait in the gallery of Mayors at the Adelaide Town Hall, in fact his is the only one missing. This almost anonymity makes the rise to Adelaide's top job of the apparently charismatic Joseph Hall even more curious.

His entry in the "S.A. Official Civic Record" of 1936 reads as follows -

"There are unfortunately very few particulars available regarding Mr. Joseph Hall, who was the third person to fill the Chief Magistracy. He was first returned to the City Council on 12th October, 1852, as Alderman for Robe Ward, and in 1854 was elected Mayor. He occupied the Chair for a year and afterwards continued in the office of Alderman until 10th February, 1857, when his death occurred. It is known that at the time of his demise he conducted the business of broker in an office in what is now known as the Waterhouse Chambers at the corner of King William and Rundle Streets, and that his private address was in Pennington

The Waterhouse Building on the corner of Rundle Mall and King William Street was built as far back as 1847. Adelaide's third Mayor, the thirsty Joseph Hall, who died during a fit of the D.T's., had his offices in this building during the early 1850s.

No doubt in Hall's time the old landmark had a much more gracious air to it than it does today with its hodge-podge of advertising signs.

Terrace, North Adelaide. He was buried in West Terrace cemetery. Mr. Hall's age appears in the cemetery records as 54 years, while on the tombstone it is given as 51 years."

That brief official account tells us little about the man himself and certainly gives no hint of his consistent colourful behaviour, or of the cause of his death. Sadly, the tombstone mentioned in the 1936 book is no longer standing and the actual location of Hall's grave cannot be pinpointed.

When he first became an Alderman all council meetings were held at the Blenheim Hotel and no doubt most council members, including Hall, imbibed a little, or a lot, at the conclusion of each meeting. Waterhouse Chambers, from where Hall worked as a broker, exists much the same today as it did when he daily climbed the staircase from King William Street. The building was erected in 1847 by Thomas Waterhouse from proceeds from the Burra Burra Mine. The Pennington Terrace home was on a large slice of land opposite today's site of Colonel Light's statue. As well as being elevated to Adelaide's top job, Joseph Hall worked and lived in top locations.

Hall had married Jane Youd, or Yond, some time prior to the couple arriving in South Australia, which was pre 1841. There is a possibility that he may have spent some time in China for among the items bequeathed to his daughter Elizabeth Jane were two Chinese tables, two Chinese work boxes, a Chinese cigar box and a Chinese tea caddy. Perhaps he simply liked oriental objects, who knows!

But back to that eventful Summer's night in Kermode Street. The performing dignitary was dressed in trousers, hat, boots and nightshirt. He was continually shouting at the crowd below, accusing them of wanting to kill him. He commenced running backwards and forwards along the verandah, encouraged by the vociferous crowd. Then someone arrived with a ladder and made an attempt to grab him. Hall lunged at the man on the ladder, dislodging him. The mob cheered as the would-be rescuer saved himself by catching on to the edge of the verandah. Then there was silence. Joseph Hall had run to the other end of the verandah and kept running, falling heavily to the street below. The fun was over.

The fall seemed to only stun him. He actually landed on his feet and kept running round in circles, asking all the time for someone to take him home. George Thompson, a North Adelaide draper and a friend of Hall's took him by the arm and accompanied by Police Constable Dennis Sullivan led him to the North Adelaide Police Station, where Sullivan felt the star of the evening's performance might sleep off the effects of whatever he had been drinking. The local Sergeant agreed and provided a suitable bed in the station-house for his distinguished guest.

That should have been the end of an eventful night but a few hours later Hall became violently ill. Dr. Charles Davies was called for. Dr. Davies lived opposite Staines' grocery shop and had been wakened earlier by the commotion in the street but when he realised it was only the former mayor making a fool of himself he simply went back to bed.

Dr. Davies arrived at the station-house in time to find Hall "in a state of near madness" and clearly at death's door. There was nothing he could do for him. He died shortly after. The jury at the ensuing coronial inquest, held at the Scotch Thistle Hotel, found that he died from "the effect of a fall from a verandah while in a state of temporary insanity". No mention was made of the fact that he was suffering from a bout of delirium tremens, even though that was confirmed several times at the inquest.

Hall had been living in the Kermode Street house as a guest of Henry Staines. He had been there for about seven weeks, apparently separated from his family across in Pennington Terrace. Various witnesses reported that during those seven weeks Joseph Hall had been drunk most of the time, having built up a good stock of wine and spirits in the cellar.

What a tragic and sad end for one of Adelaide's early leading citizens.

2

The Sad Old Mill
on Windmill Hill

The sign at the top of Windmill Hill on the Old Mount Barker Road between Hahndorf and Mount Barker is a little confusing. It points to 'Old Nixon's Mill'. Now, is that a mill belonging to old Nixon, or is it an old mill belonging to Nixon? Judging from its present condition it looks as though it doesn't belong to anybody and that's a shame, for old Nixon's Mill, or Nixon's old mill, has a colourful and interesting past. It also looked a lot more attractive not that many years ago.

The mill certainly is old, it was built in 1842 and the man who erected it was named Nixon, so that clears up the enigmatic sign. Nixon was in fact a member of Colonel Light's survey team. He had been involved in the surveying of the Mount Barker district and the area must have appealed to him for he elected to change his occupational course by purchasing land and becoming the district's first miller.

Nixon was not however the first in the Adelaide Hills for an earlier mill had been built by John Dunn the year before, across to the north-east in the Hay Valley. Dunn later constructed the wonderful water-powered Bridgewater Mill, in 1853.

Another mill made its appearance not far away about the same time as Nixon's. That one was built by the junction of Cox's Creek and the Onkaparinga River by German settler Friedrich Wittwer. There were also a few down on the plains so the colony's milling industry was well and truly up and running within those first five years of settlement.

Nixon did not remain a miller for very long for by 1844 he had sold out to Walter Paterson for two hundred and fifty pounds. We can only speculate whether the sale was prompted by a chance to make a profit, an unsuitable choice of profession, the isolated existence or even trouble with the natives.

The original inhabitants of the Mount Barker area were from all reports a relatively peaceful group. It must have been traumatic for them when the white invaders took over their home ground but there is little evidence of any major retaliation. There are on the other hand accounts

The restored Mount Barker mill photographed in 1970.

It was built in 1842 and remained in use until 1864, succumbing to the more reliable water and steam powered mills coming into use. At one stage in its short history as a working mill a fierce battle was fought beside it between warring native tribes. The miller, Walter Paterson, locked his family inside the mill and unsuccessfully attempted to mediate.

of occasional battles with the tribes from the Murray River to the east and from the Encounter Bay district to the south. Those two tribes were apparently quite troublesome to Europeans, to each other and to their Mount Barker neighbours.

The inter-tribal fighting was some times over the stealing of women, usually resulting in the retrieval of the unfortunate young lady and the punishment of the perpetrators of the crime. There were of course many other causes as well, such as boundary disputes and thieving from each other and it would seem, from the number of reported incidents, that general animosity between the tribes had existed for a very long time.

Shortly after Walter Paterson took over Nixon's mill there were several

*As the Mount Barker mill
looked in 1999, back once
again to its derelict condition.*

battles between the native neighbours and some of the fighting took place around Mount Barker.

One such incident took place on Cro' Nest Hill, to the east of the settlement. A Mount Barker man had induced a Murray River girl to move to the hills and the river people objected. They came after her, fully armed with their spears, boomerangs and waddies. The subsequent fighting was broken up by a detachment of troopers who had been summoned by a native woman. She afterwards received a spear right through her body for her trouble and died as a result. The police eventually restored order and the young lady at the centre of the dispute returned to the river.

A similar battle took place across by Walter Paterson's mill between the local men and those from Encounter Bay. The reason may have only been a long-standing grudge but the southerners meant business, arriving in their frightening warpaint and fully armed. The Mount Barker men were well prepared and apparently matched their attackers in determination to come out victors. Paterson locked his family in the safety of the solid mill and with the assistance of a few friends did what he could to prevent too much bloodshed but achieved little due to the numbers involved. The miller and his helpers were forced to become spectators to a very fierce free-for-all with many injuries being inflicted to both sides. The arrival of troopers finally ended the fighting, well, that round of it anyway.

The old mill changed hands a third time in 1853. It was sold by Walter Paterson to Friedrich Wittwer who had abandoned his earlier mill by the Onkaparinga and established another at Hahndorf. The wind-driven mill of Nixon/Paterson/Wittwer ceased functioning in 1864 as others powered by water and steam proved more reliable.

Over the years it became a derelict ruin. Eventually, under the control of the Mount Barker Council, the sails were returned to the stone tower and with other repairs it became a delightful attraction for travellers on the old highway through the hills. These days the mill has once again faded into disrepair, the sails are gone and whatever would-be admirers there might have been now speed by at a distance on the Southern Expressway.

3   *Fry's Clump*

O ne of the most unexpected roadside memorials in South Australia is to be found near Balaclava, a few kilometres out of town on the way to Owen. The memorial itself is not unusual, just a plaque set in a stone, it is what is being remembered that seems so strange. We read plenty of inscriptions commemorating first happenings, heroic deeds, symbolic sites, etc. but it certainly is rare to find one proclaiming that this is the place where one of our early pioneer pastoralists murdered his wife. It becomes even more surprising when one reads that the memorial was a Bicentennial project. Well, why not! History covers past events in general and not just those touched by important people or places. No doubt this memorial creates just as much interest to passers-by as one that features a programmed act by a dull politician.

> *"This memorial was erected*
> *in the bicentennial year*
> *so all may know that*
> *this area of native scrub is called*
> *"FRY'S CLUMP"*
> *as pioneer pastoralist Robert Fry*
> *is said to have murdered his wife here in January 1850.*
> *five months later*
> *his remains were found nearby".*

A catchy name, Fry's Clump. One would imagine Robert Fry would have preferred having a mountain, or a river, or a township named after him. Still, it is a unique honour, there can't be too many people memorialised with a clump.

So, who was this man destined for such recognition? He was probably the 22-year-old Robert Fry who arrived in South Australia, along with his 19-year-old wife, on the "Buckinghamshire" in 1838. The young man was a shepherd from Woodchester, in Gloucestershire. Shortly after arrival he was engaged as an agricultural labourer by Mr. R. J. Bourchier, a fellow passenger on the "Buckinghamshire".

There would not be too many memorials around Australia to locations where early settlers murdered their wives. This unusual one near Balaclava in South Australia's mid-north is certainly unique. A later owner of the land placed a condition on future sales that the murder site must never be cleared.

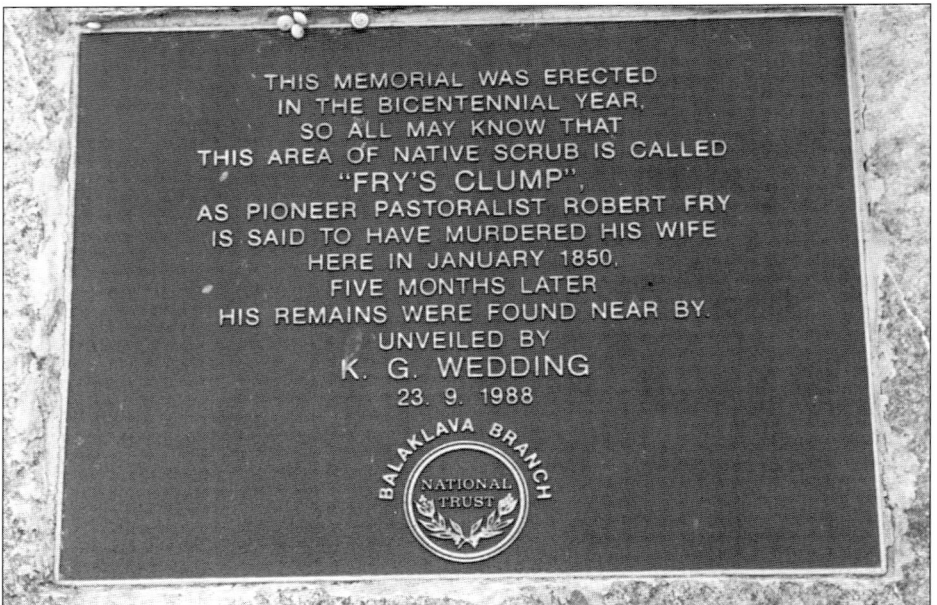

THIS MEMORIAL WAS ERECTED
IN THE BICENTENNIAL YEAR,
SO ALL MAY KNOW THAT
THIS AREA OF NATIVE SCRUB IS CALLED
"FRY'S CLUMP",
AS PIONEER PASTORALIST ROBERT FRY
IS SAID TO HAVE MURDERED HIS WIFE
HERE IN JANUARY 1850.
FIVE MONTHS LATER
HIS REMAINS WERE FOUND NEAR BY.
UNVEILED BY
K. G. WEDDING
23. 9. 1988

BALAKLAVA BRANCH
NATIONAL TRUST

We next hear of him at Islington and selling milk in Adelaide and a few years after that at McLaren Vale and then Yankalila. By that time Robert Fry was beginning to prosper and already had 90 cattle, some pigs and was growing wheat. The move to the Wakefield River district near today's Balaclava came in the mid 1840s when he was granted an occupational licence for a considerable stretch of land. In 1847 he appears there as a dairyman but by 1850 classed himself as a stockholder, and indeed he was for he now boasted 500 head of cattle as well as 20 or 30 horses.

Robert and Louisa Fry by then had three children, aged from 8 down to 18 months. Another baby had died in infancy in 1844. The family was typical of several beginning to become established in what was at the time still a sparsely populated area of the mid north of South Australia.

The first news of the murder of Louisa Fry reached Adelaide on January 11th, 1850 when a local Justice of the Peace reported the tragic event to the Colonial Secretary. He stated that he had been directed to a site close to the Fry home and had seen the corpse of Mrs. Fry lying across the bottom of the family gig and covered with cushions and curtains. The remains were in a dreadful decomposed state so he had arranged for the body to be wrapped in a blanket and buried there and then in an enlarged rabbit hole. A policeman from Clare had been summoned and requested to remain at the gravesite should Mr. Fry return home for he was suspected of carrying out the atrocity. It was known locally that Robert Fry had been in an unstable state of mind for some time and had actually attempted suicide not long before at Ladd's Inn at Gepps Cross.

Sergeant-Major McCulloch was placed in charge of a party of police called in from Kooringa and they set out in pursuit of Robert Fry. They searched the area widely for several weeks without success and received only one worthwhile lead, that some natives had seen the wanted man in the bush near the top of the Gulf. Bushfires swept the countryside around the Wakefield at the time and it was thought that Fry had little chance of surviving. The search was eventually called off.

The only family the Frys had in South Australia was Louisa's cousin, Mrs. Mary Ann Bird of Glenelg. Mr. Bird immediately travelled north to the property to take care of things and to arrange a more decent burial for his wife's relative. The children had been found in a poorly state at the house and were being looked after temporarily by Dr. Webb of Clare. They were taken back to Glenelg to the care of Mrs. Bird but the youngest died a few months later.

Nothing more happened for several months. It was in fact McCulloch who finally made the discovery that closed the case. One day in late June he was poking about the bush about half a mile from the murder site when he stumbled onto human bones. They were scattered over a considerable area and clothing nearby had been torn to pieces by wild animals. A rifle, a pistol, a notebook, a cutting knife and a bonnet later identified as Mrs. Fry's all combined to confirm that Robert Fry had been found.

An inquest was held at the Port Henry Arms Hotel and it was agreed that Fry had taken his wife's life and afterwards committed suicide. His remains were then interred in the cemetery across at Penwortham. The property, known as Fry's Run, was placed in trust for the three children but was eventually sold to James White of Kapunda. It was held from 1890 to 1946 by F. Waegener. A condition of the 1890 purchase was that the patch of scrub known as "Fry's Clump" was never to be cleared.

The condition has been honoured through the years and the permanent stone memorial is bound to ensure that "Fry's Clump" will remain where it is for many years to come.

4

Ding Dong Dell, Martin's in the Well

Water – the most precious of all commodities, certainly to Adelaide's first settlers. Back 'home' the supply of water had never been a great problem. The majority could simply fill their buckets as needed from the village well, or nearby brook. There was no reliable communal well in Adelaide and the nearby brook, the Torrens, failed to flow during summer months and became nothing more than a succession of pools.

Many inhabitants of the city obtained their water from professional water carriers and by the late 1840s were paying up to 3/- a load. This was drawn from the Torrens and the quality and taste of that taken from the summer pools would only add to the general misery caused by the exorbitant price.

Most residents dug shallow wells on their properties and of course saved whatever water that could be saved from the run-off from roofs but neither method came close to fulfilling their requirements. Some really deep wells would supply continual water but the quality was always a problem.

Many thoughts were put forward as to the best method of instituting a regular supply of pure water to Adelaide. Most suggestions concerned the creeks coming down from the hills. Dams would be needed and waterwheels were envisaged at various stages to keep the flow moving along open troughs across the plain to the city. Something would have to be done, one day!

The water carriers gave the City Commissioners a few headaches in April 1850 and with their behaviour brought emphasis to the urgent need for theorising about the supply of water to be turned to action. The carriers actually went out on strike. Needless to say, the suffering public were not amused.

Their unpopular action resulted from a decision made by the Commissioners to re-build the ford across the Torrens to North Adelaide. This was urgently needed as past winters had resulted in the crossing being out of action for several weeks and more and more traffic was now using the ford. The first thing to be done was divert the flow to enable dry access to the site. This resulted in the spot becoming a stagnant pond, which quickly turned into a boggy mess as traffic continued through it.

It was from that part of the river the carriers drew the town's supply and they were convinced there was no other suitable point for their carts to enter the stream. They approached the authorities and requested that the new embankment be cut across, thus allowing some water to flow through to the old filling place but the Commissioners refused to co-operate.

So, one by one, fifty water carriers backed their water carts all the way down King William Street to the open acre between the Post Office and the Exchange building. They shouted out their story of how the Commissioners were slowly poisoning the citizens of Adelaide and all over each cart were hastily prepared placards bearing the pointed message – 'NO WATER'

Many speeches followed and as a conclusion three hearty hisses were given for the Governor, Sir Henry Young. By the end of the eventful day, and after several more excursions including a march on the office of the Colonial Secretary, Charles Sturt, the authorities finally relented and issued a statement – 'The water will be re-directed'. Another mini-crisis had passed in the infant colony.

Adelaide finally received its first regular water supply in 1860, under pressure from the newly-built Thorndon Park reservoir, filled in turn from a weir on the Torrens Gorge.

Water was gradually connected to homes and businesses throughout the town and hundreds of wells of all shapes and sizes and depths became obsolete. Some of course remained in use for many years and there are even wells from those early days that are still used. One in particular is interesting for a multitude of people pass it every day without being aware of it. The well was dug in 1855 in the Botanic Garden to supply water during the establishment of that Adelaide showpiece. There is no outward hint of the existence of this relic from the pioneering days. Today it is simply covered by a square of heavy iron but the sound of a motor beneath reveals its continued use. The old well is on the western side of the Wisteria Arbor, by the edge of the Plane Tree Lawn.

Not far away, a little to the east of the futuristic Bicentennial Conservatory, is another old well that possibly dates from the same period. This is on land formerly occupied by the State Transport Authority and where the International Rose Garden has been created. The large, unlined well was uncovered in 1995 when an old tram barn was demolished. A huge slab of concrete had been placed over it. How long the well was there before the tram barn was built is a matter of conjecture but the odds are that it dates back to when the area was the orchard of the Adelaide Lunatic Asylum. The well has now been lined with cement piping and grilled over and has become a feature in one section of the new Rose Garden.

There are scores of other historic wells around South Australia that have interesting histories. The best known would probably be Chinaman's Well, to the south of Salt Creek, on the Coorong.

Chinaman's Well very probably pre-dated European and Oriental newcomers but it is believed that it received its singular stone-lined bottle-

Chinaman's Well, south of Salt Creek, very probably pre-dated European and Oriental newcomers but it is believed that it received its singular stone-lined bottle-top shape and limestone lining around the late 1850s to become one of a series of watering places to service Chinese travellers. The Chinese were moving along the Coorong track in great numbers on their way from Robe to the Victorian goldfields.

One of the two wells at Two Wells. Direction to their location became the name of the township that grew around them.

top shape and limestone lining around the late 1850s to become one of a series of watering places to service Chinese travellers. The Chinese were moving along the Coorong track in great numbers on their way to the Victorian goldfields. The imposition of a discouraging landing tax in Victoria prompted many sea captains to offload their celestial passengers at South Australia's Robe, from where they were forced to walk the long distance into Victoria. It is estimated that the number who landed at Robe between 1857 and 1863 was as high as 16,000.

Other equally well-known wells are a couple to the north of Adelaide where the direction to their location became the name of the township that grew around them – Two Wells. They, like scores of others around the state, were originally native wells that were taken over by European settlers and travellers. The two were lined with stone and given a windlass and accompanying trough during the 1880s but eventually fell into disuse. In recent times they have been given new walls and one a windlass, the other a shelter.

To the east of Adelaide, at Peake, is a well with a puzzling name, Polly's Well. It is believed that Polly was the name of the wife of a local settler – or the name of a horse used regularly in drawing water from it – or the name of a cow that fell in it! These old watering places and campsites all had their own descriptive names and a study of today's maps will reveal scores of intriguing names to ponder over.

Back in the CBD of Adelaide old wells are hidden away all over the place. It would be nice to know if Dr. Nash's well in Grenfell Street is still intact under one of the mammoth modern buildings for it featured in a remarkable survival story back about the time of the water carriers dispute.

Josiah Martin, a boarding-house keeper of Grenfell Street, was returning home late one evening quite inebriated and had difficulty locating his front door. He stumbled towards the home of his neighbour Dr. Nash and did not notice the Doctor's 80ft well. In he tumbled, taking what seemed to be an eternity before reaching the bottom. He recalled

Polly's Well at Peake. It is believed that Polly might have been the name of the wife of a local settler – or the name of a horse used regularly in drawing water from it – or the name of a cow that fell in it.

later that on the way down he was convinced the Devil had grabbed him. Martin was very fortunate that the water in the well only reached his knees. Still not having any real notion as to where he was, he began a series of doleful howlings. Luckily Dr. Nash heard Martin bewailing his deep and watery berth and went to his assistance with a long rope. Several men were finally needed to get him to the surface and all were astounded to find that he suffered no more than a few scratches, an amazing thing considering the depth he fell.

Martin's rescuers all agreed they had witnessed a strong recommendation for the excessive consumption of alcohol while Martin himself vowed he would never touch another drop.

5

Plants and Creatures
Great and Small

The Adelaide Botanic Garden opened its gates to the public in September 1857 and within months application was made to Government for extra funds so that a small zoo could be created in the Garden. The application failed. Nevertheless, members of the public began donating the odd swan, or duck, then an owl, then more ducks and all were accepted. After all, it was what the public wanted, the lake had been formed and a small aviary or two could easily be put together by the Garden staff. Problems commenced however when people began bringing in wallabies and wombats. Their feeding and housing had to take second place to the maintenance and continuing development of the Garden itself and funds were very tight.

So, in May 1859 another approach was made, the all clear received and a small budget created. An advertisement was placed in the 'Advertiser' announcing that "preparations have been made for the introduction into the Garden of waterfowl and other birds and interesting harmless little-known animals and that contributions were sought with all charges of conveyance being cheerfully paid".

This brought a flood of response and so began what was to become a very large zoo in the Botanic Garden. Within a relatively short time the collection of "harmless little-known animals" included bears, tigers, lion cubs, baboons, snakes, llamas, camels and a Brahmin bull. One wonders how the gardeners reacted and coped when some of the new additions arrived. The animals remained as an integral part of the garden's display until the early 1880s when they were transferred to the adjacent newly-created Zoological Gardens. Not all the birds went at that time. Several aviaries continued to house their colourful and cheerful residents within the Botanic Garden for many years.

At one period during the very early days of the Garden zoo there was a great controversy and much finger pointing when four ducks were found dead and a pair of parent swans attacked and killed their four

When the beautiful Palm House was built in Adelaide's Botanic Garden in 1877 its neighbouring building was the monkey house. No doubt the calls of the monkeys from across the way would have added something to the tropical experience of a visit to the Palm House.

offspring before suddenly dying themselves. The swans were considered quite valuable as they were the first of their breed to have been brought into the colony. The Director of the Garden, George Francis, was furious. He immediately placed the blame on Mr. Burford of Grenfell Street. Francis publicly declared that arsenic emanating from Burford's candle manufacturing plant had found its way through the city sewers and into the lake.

That really upset Mr. Burford. He counter-claimed that perhaps Francis himself was to blame. He argued that maybe Francis had laid baits for dogs coming into the Garden and somehow the swans and ducks got to it first. The real cause was never really established but the ever-so-special swans were eventually stuffed for posterity.

Such mini dramas occurred from time to time as dogs were always getting in and attacking animals, the public were often accused of harassing the poorly-caged creatures and accidents happened occasionally to both visitors and garden staff. Some accidents were serious, such as the time William Whitehead, a boy in the employ of the Garden, was savagely attacked by a monkey. Young William spent several weeks recuperating in the Adelaide Hospital next door.

The monkey house was quite large. It stood where today's kiosk is located. When the beautiful Palm House was built in 1877 its neighbouring building was the monkey house and no doubt the calls of the monkeys from across the way would have added something to the tropical experience of a visit to the Palm House.

By this lovely old tree in Adelaide's Botanic Garden there once were enclosures housing tigers, bears and other large creatures. This was the area for the big animals of the Garden's zoo which existed for over 20 years, until the early 1880s.

The majestic River Red Gum is estimated to be over 250 years old. It is one of a few examples of remnant vegetation of the Adelaide plains surviving within the Botanic Garden.

In 1867 a pair of Tasmanian Devils were acquired by the Adelaide Botanic Garden. Being the first to be brought into the colony they were expected to become a major attraction. But disaster stuck. One escaped on arrival at Port Adelaide and the other escaped in the city. The Port Adelaide escapee was never seen again but the city fugitive was sighted a fortnight later at Glen Osmond.

As time went by the little Devils were forgotten about – until six years later when one of them, no doubt the Glen Osmond traveller, was trapped near Mount Lofty. Who knows, had the pair escaped together, today the Mount Lofty Range might be overrun with Tasmanian Devils.

There was one unusual happening some years earlier that could have had an interesting result. In early 1867 Dr. Schomburgk, the then Director, travelled to the eastern colonies on a collecting expedition. He visited both Sydney and Melbourne and returned with a large quantity of plants and seeds, as well as a pair of Tasmanian Devils, a male and a female.

Disaster struck when he landed with his treasures at Port Adelaide. One of the little Devils escaped. Then, to add to the Doctor's embarrassment, the other escaped on arrival at the Botanic Garden. Two very rare and valuable Tasmanian Devils were loose, one at the Port and one in the city. Pleas were placed in the newspapers requesting colonists not to destroy the strange animals if sighted but to attempt a capture, and if successful, return the fugitives to the Botanic Garden.

The first glimpses of hope came a fortnight later when one was seen at Glen Osmond. It quickly disappeared into the bush and despite a thorough search of the immediate area was not seen again. Time went by and there were no more sightings. The adventures of the Tasmanian Devils were eventually forgotten as more important and impressive accomplishments of Dr. Schomburgk rightfully gained the public's attention.

Six years later, in 1873, a most amazing thing occurred near Piccadilly, on a property very close to today's Mount Lofty Botanic Garden. A settler, Mr. Schocroft, trapped a very strange animal. Neither he nor any of his neighbours had ever seen anything like it before. He decided to take it down to Adelaide to see if Dr. Schomburgk could identify it and, if he so desired, accept the funny but ferocious looking little fellow as an exhibit in the Botanic Garden.

Dr. Schomburgk could hardly believe his eyes. He immediately identified the captive as a Tasmanian Devil and declared that he was convinced it was the one that had escaped from the Garden way back in 1867. He willingly accepted Mr. Schocroft's offer and the little Devil finally took up residence in the Botanic Garden.

Nothing more was ever heard of the Port Adelaide escapee. Who knows, if the two had both escaped from the Garden and headed to the hills together perhaps the Mount Lofty Range might today be overrun with their descendants. The little fellow might then not have led such a devil of an existence in South Australia.

6   *Riotous Behaviour*

A delaide ... even the lovely name conjures up dreamy images of peace, of boats on the Torrens, of children playing in the parks and gardens, of soft tolling of bells, of sunny days on crowded beaches, of bustling streetside cafes, of happy faces and cheerful greetings. Adelaide is a city of quiet beauty and the provider of a lifestyle the envy of city dwellers around the world. Turmoil and ugliness are for others. Well ... perhaps not always. Should we turn the clock back to two particular months in the city's history, to March 1870 and January 1931, we would be confronted with an entirely different image.

They were the months of the riots. Two particular periods when Adelaide showed she had a dark side, that she could be something other than the serene 'City of Churches'. The incidents happened sixty one years apart yet were in fact quite similar. Both stemmed from problems created through unacceptable unemployment and in each case an angry mob took over Victoria Square and swarmed around the Treasury Building.

The 1931 riot was quite nasty. Almost 3000 work-hungry men, some armed with iron bars, sticks and stones, fought a fierce street battle with a large complement of police, who were armed only with batons. Some of the makeshift weapons were deadly, being sticks studded with nails. The protesters had more than a peaceful demonstration on their minds.

The fateful day began with about 50 or 60 members of the Waterside Workers Federation and Seaman's Union congregating at Port Adelaide and setting off to march all the way to the city. Their main intention was to protest against the Government for omitting beef from the ration issue for the unemployed. The leaders carried large red flags and placards bearing pointed messages and the whole group sang 'The Red Flag' as they stepped it out up the Port Road. All harmless enough at that point.

By the time the procession reached Woodville its size had doubled and it was when they reached Southwark that things altered. About one thousand unemployed had marched from the Labor Exchange in the city to join forces with their Port Adelaide brethren and brought with them

The Treasury Building, Victoria Square, Adelaide, the scene of two vicious riots, sixty-one years apart.

On May 1st, 1870 a large group of desperate unemployed men assembled opposite the Treasury Building and, as a journalist of the day reported, 'mischief was intended'. The building was subsequently stormed by the mob and following their ejection a riot resulted in Victoria Square.

In January 1931 history repeated itself when another riot took place outside the Treasury Building, once again, the result of unemployment.

the array of homemade weaponry. All available mounted and foot police had escorted the threatening mob to Southwark, without incident. It was as the combined marchers headed back towards the city that the first ugliness erupted, a mounted constable was struck with a placard. Common-sense prevailed and there was no further immediate provocation from either side. The noisy procession began moving along North Terrace and as the men progressively passed Parliament House they echoed bursts of hooting and chants of the names of various members of Parliament. On they went, down King William Street, gathering numbers as they marched. The police were becoming nervous for there were far too many men now being caught up in the hysteria.

The first major confrontation came outside the Treasury Building. There the leaders spoke to the police guarding the entrance and demanded an audience with the Premier. The mob had spread out behind them, across Victoria Square and up and down Flinders Street. They were clearly becoming impatient. Then, without warning, several bricks were hurled at the policemen who had lined up outside the building. One of the constabulary received a broken jaw from a direct hit.

The brick throwing seemed to be the signal that sparked the next move. Waving their sticks and whatever else they had on hand, the demonstrators surged upon the police in open attack. The baton-waving police defended themselves and blood flowed freely in Victoria Square. Combatants and onlookers were battered, knocked down, trampled on and rendered senseless. And the Premier looked on from an upstairs window, deciding it was not the time to make an appearance.

The need to get the many injured people to hospital eventually took priority and the fighting eased. Gradually the rioters dispersed, nothing but mayhem having been achieved. The unrest however did not stop there for the same evening saw more riotous behaviour at Port Adelaide. Shop windows were smashed, stones were thrown at police and more injuries resulted.

The police, both in the city and at Port Adelaide, made several arrests and a handful of ringleaders were duly charged and gaoled. The Premier subsequently gave an audience to a small deputation but granted nothing because of the trouble they had caused. The men were then granted permission to take their grievances to the Minister of Local Government but he refused to listen to what they had to say when one man stubbornly refused to remove his hat.

And with that high-hatted attitude prevailing from both sides the process of sorting out the major issues dragged on for some time.

Sixty one years earlier, in 1870, the then labelled 'Unemployed Disturbance in King William Street' resulted from the unemployed being offered a pittance to trench the Lunatic Asylum paddock.

Around mid-day on May 1st a large group of men assembled opposite the Treasury Building and, as a journalist of the day reported, 'mischief was intended'. The police were summoned but not enough of them arrived in time to prevent the mob rushing en masse into the Government Offices, climbing the staircase, shouting and vowing vengeance against the Government. The police who were there attempted to stop the stampede but failed. Civil servants came to the rescue. They poured out of offices up and down the corridors to assist the police and after much wrestling and fisticuffs the intruders were successfully ejected and the doors bolted.

The frustrated mob now grew in size as sympathizers honed in on Victoria Square. They hassled the Commissioner of Public Works who bravely confronted them outside the door of the Treasury Building. The Commissioner of Police came to his rescue and the two were possibly saved from personal injury by the belated appearance of the mounted police, who promptly lined up in front of the building. A stalemate. Who was going to make the next move?

Rumblings went through the crowd. A suggestion circulated that some of the city stores should be rushed and about a hundred men formed into ranks in the middle of the Square with that intention. Orders however became confused and their plans were thwarted when the troopers realised what was afoot. So, instead of marching through the streets the men marched across to the vacant space by the Town Hall where one of the leaders stood on a mud-cart and addressed the crowd. He encouraged all pick and shovel men present to get their tools, re-assemble in half-an-hour and demand work or bread, and to be assured that if it came to pass, they would get food and lodgings in the gaol which they were unable to get at that moment under present conditions.

About fifty men turned up and began the trek back towards the Treasury Building. Twenty police barred the doorway but they were promptly pushed aside and attempts then made to bash down the locked door. A melee erupted and the mounted troopers closed in. In time the crowd was broken up, only to re-assemble outside the Post Office. The troopers had the upper hand during the fighting as they were using the flat of their swords, aimed at the shoulders and arms of the stone-throwing protesters. Needless to say, more than one man received a deep gash across the head. The fight continued outside the Post Office but eventually the police won the day and arrested the ringleaders, the others quickly disappearing down back streets.

The outcome of the disturbance was that the 'pittance' originally offered for trenching at the Asylum, 1/10d per day, was raised to 3/- per day and should that prove insufficient to support any man with a large family, extra rations would be granted. In this case, violence had paid off.

The men who had instigated the trouble were however punished and several were gaoled. One evening a rumour circulated that a gaol-break was being planned to release the rioters and the Government responded by swearing-in 33 special constables to boost the police numbers. Nothing eventuated. The ringleaders served their full terms in prison and the needy men enjoyed their revised terms of temporary employment at the Lunatic Asylum.

7 *Three Bridges to Nowhere*

Old bridges that have been bypassed by modern roads and highways can be found all over South Australia. Some are in complete disrepair, a number have been restored and a few have kept their original condition. Most of them, no matter what their state, retain an air of romantic beauty, particularly the old stone arched bridges, several of which were built throughout the Adelaide Hills. One of the most beautiful crosses the Deep Creek in a steep gully not far from Basket Range. Atmosphere abounds. On a wintry, foggy morning a visitor to the Deep Creek bridge could be excused for imagining hearing strains of 'Brigadoon' and seeing dim figures from the past dancing through the mist.

The bridge is well away from the road these days. Glimpses of it can be seen at certain points as you wind your way towards Basket Range from Ashton. From a distance it looks to be in good condition, and it is. The Deep Creek bridge was fully restored during the early 1990s as a joint project by the District Council of East Torrens, involving the East Torrens Historical Society, and the Department of Employment, Education and Training. A commendable and successful exercise, despite the fact that the bridge goes nowhere, it is simply a monument to the past.

It was first built in 1867 and was last used in 1913, when the present road was constructed. The road from Magill to Lobethal was completed around 1870 and the building of the bridge over the Deep Creek with its dramatically steep banks had been one of the major hurdles to overcome. Norwood contractor Alfred Adams constructed the bridge at a cost of two hundred and fifty pounds and his problems must have been enormous considering the bridge's location and the obvious difficulties in transporting the necessary stone.

Adams had other problems around that time. Shortly after the Deep Creek bridge was completed he gained a contract with the Railways Department that led to personal financial losses. The situation he found himself in became too heavy a burden to carry and Adams took his own life, near Kapunda, in early 1871. At the time he was working on the River

Light bridge. There was an old public house nearby and it was there, during a fit of deep depression, that the troubled man sharpened a kitchen knife and cut his own throat.

The romantic Deep Creek bridge now remains as a solemn monument to a talented but tragic bridge builder.

A totally different bridge to nowhere crosses the Onkaparinga close to Woodside. It sits beside a branch road that also has the appearance of leading to nowhere. This bridge is a wooden one and is surely the quaintest old swing bridge to be found in South Australia.

It is no longer crossable, officially anyway. There is a ford nearby and always has been, the bridge meant for pedestrians, for times of flash flooding and for use during those months of the year when the Onkaparinga becomes too high for safe crossing of the ford.

Over a hundred years ago there were in fact five such swing bridges crossing the Onkaparinga in the Woodside/Oakbank area, the Woodside relic now being the only survivor. One of the five was suspended over the

The building of the Deep Creek bridge near Basket Range was a wonderful achievement back in 1867. The builder of the bridge, Alfred Adams, overcame many problems in completing the contract but could not overcome financial difficulties that followed a few years later. He committed suicide in 1871.

One hundred years ago there were five of these swing bridges over the Onkaparinga in the Woodside/Oakbank area, now only one remains. The old monument to the past is just out of Woodside and has survived many part demolitions due to floods. The above photo was taken immediately after a flood in 1992. The bridge was shortly after repaired once again.

river by the Oakbank brewery but after a couple of replacements due to flood damage that was dismantled and the level of the adjoining ford raised. Stories survive from the days of the Oakbank bridge. At the time of one early Oakbank race meeting the Onkaparinga flooded and the bridge was partly demolished. Racegoers became stranded on the wrong side of the river. Cabbies took advantage of the situation and physically carried willing passengers across at a shilling a time, thus saving many a fashionable dress from imagined disaster.

The remaining old masterpiece of carpentry, the Woodside bridge, was itself all but destroyed by floods in 1992. Fortunately the Onkaparinga Council and Army personnel from the Woodside barracks combined to restore the district's ageing treasure. And so, as with the restored Deep Creek bridge, we have another delightful monument to the past to admire and ponder over without expecting it to take us anywhere.

The third bridge to nowhere cannot be visited for it is now only a memory. It really never became a bridge to anywhere but a bridge it was, and a big one at that.

In early 1865 the Director of Adelaide's Botanic Garden, George Francis, convinced the Board of Governors that a bridge was needed to span the newly created ornamental pond at the bottom of the main walk down from North Terrace. An order was subsequently sent to London and a master plan of paths, garden beds, tree plantings, etc. was worked on in anticipation of the arrival of the bridge, expected to happen well within the year.

The big day finally came in September of 1866. No doubt there was much excitement as arrangements were made for the bridge to be offloaded at Port Adelaide and transported to the Botanic Garden. It was of course in pieces, in kit form, and a complicated assembly process was anticipated. What was not anticipated was that someone had blundered.

When all the unpacking of iron rods, bars, girders, bolts, etc. had been completed it became apparent that what they had was a bridge large enough to span the Torrens. Francis had died just a few months after the order had been placed and his successor, Dr. Richard Schomburgk, inherited the problem. It could not be determined if the error had been made in the ordering, the interpretation of the order or in the bridge's despatch. Despite several searches through the files of various Government Departments, the original plans of the proposed pond bridge could not be located.

The Government washed its hands of the matter. It was, they declared, the Botanic Garden's problem and it was up to them to sort it out. Attempts were then made to sell the oversized bridge to the Government, to replace the ageing Frome Road footbridge across the river, but that fell on deaf ears. Over ensuing months many other attempts were made to sell their white elephant to various municipal bodies but nobody wanted it. And so, for years to come, an immense pile of iron bits and pieces lay beside the river bank in Botanic Park simply rusting away.

In June 1882, sixteen years after its arrival, a last-ditch attempt was made to find a use for the bridge. At that time the Acclimatisation Society was pressuring the Botanic Garden for the release of some of its land so that the former could create a new Zoological Garden. The Botanic Garden Board objected strongly to the thought of relinquishing any portion of their allotted space and suggested that the proposed new zoo should be situated on the opposite side of the Torrens, at the location of the old Botanic Garden, and, if that was acceptable, they could even supply a bridge to span the Torrens for easy access. The suggestion was ignored and they were eventually forced to give up land for the zoo.

The end of the embarrassing saga came thirty three years after the bridge's arrival when the Board of the Botanic Garden accepted forty two pounds for what was by then just a heap of rusty scrap iron. Perhaps we have similar examples today of mismanagement of the public purse but the debacle of the Botanic Garden bridge to nowhere, which originally cost the taxpayers of South Australia six hundred pounds, would be hard to match.

8   *When the 'Hero of Niagara' Came to Adelaide*

Waterfall Gully, Adelaide Oval, the Parklands and the Torrens Lake, they all have something in common. Well, of course they do, they are some of Adelaide's premier beauty spots. But what else? Is there some notable person or persons, or perhaps a curious happening or two, that links the beauty spots? The answer is yes. The magical name Blondin drew thousands to the locations during the latter half of the nineteenth century to be thrilled and dazzled by extraordinary daredevil entertainment.

Who was Blondin? He was a Frenchman, Jean Francois Gravelet, born in 1824. By the age of 5 his parents had introduced him to the exciting life of the theatre and billed as 'The Little Wonder' he was amazing enthralled audiences with unusual gymnastic performances. He was so good that his acts became a leading feature at principal theatres throughout Paris.

Gravelet stayed on in the theatre and his career blossomed. He adopted the name Blondin and at the age of 21 crossed to America where he quickly made a name for himself as a tightrope walker. In 1859 he attempted something that no-one had even dared to contemplate before – he crossed Niagara Falls on a tightrope. It was estimated that 50,000 onlookers assembled on the allotted day to witness the 'lunatic' attempt the impossible – which he did with ease.

The little Frenchman did not rest there. Widespread adulation by the American and Canadian public drove him on and a few months later he returned to Niagara to walk the wire again, this time blindfolded and wrapped in a heavy sack. That was followed by the amazing and amusing act of pushing a wheelbarrow across. The public wanted more and he kept returning with further breathtaking performances. They included turning somersaults as he ambled along the rope, walking the distance dressed as a slave in shackles and carrying a man all the way across on his back. Then the most spectacular of all, Blondin walked the Niagara rope

BLONDIN,
THE
HERO OF NIAGARA,
WILL MAKE HIS
FIRST GRAND
HIGH ROPE ASCENSION,
ON SATURDAY, FEBRUARY 6, 1875,
in his
GIGANTIC ARENA, SOUTH PARK LANDS,
The dimensions of which far surpass any other
canvas enclosure in the World.
The Performance will include the same
WONDERFUL FEATS
as performed by him over the
GIGANTIC FALLS OF NIAGARA,
in America, in the presence of
H.R.H. the PRINCE OF WALES and SUITE,
including
His Grace the Duke of Newcastle, Earl St.
Germain, the Marquis of Chandos, Lord Lyons,
General Williams, Major Teesdale, Major-
General Bruce, and many other distinguished
Noblemen and Gentlemen.
N.B.—For the convenience of the public, and
to prevent crowding, the doors will be opened at
half-past 4 p.m.
By general request, in consequence of the heat
in the earlier part of the day, the performance
will commence at 6 p.m. sharp.
Carriages may be ordered at quarter past 7
o'clock.
Prices of Admission—First class Seats, 5s.,
Children under 12 years, 2s. 6d. Second-class,
Promenade, 2s. 6d., Children under 12, 1s.
No readmission.

SOUTH AUSTRALIAN RAILWAYS.

BLONDIN'S OPENING DAY, SATURDAY,
FEBRUARY 6.
NORTH LINE.
EXCURSION RETURN TICKETS at
SINGLE FARES will be issued on Saturday,
6th February, for 1st, 2nd, and 3rd Class Pas-
sengers at all Stations on the North Line for
Adelaide, available for return up to and by the
4 30 p.m. Train on MONDAY, the 8th February.

PORT LINE.
EXCURSION RETURN TICKETS at
SINGLE FARES will be issued on Saturday,
the 6th February, for 1st, 2nd, and 3rd Class
Passengers, at all Stations on the Port Line for
Adelaide, available for return same day only.
(See Railway Advertisement).

Letters and communications to be addressed
to J. F. Blondin; or C. P. Niaud, Secretary,
Prince Alfred Hotel, King William-street.
By order
LE CHEVALIER BLONDIN,
H. P. LYONS, Agent.
NOTICE.
TO THE INHABITANTS OF THE SUR-
ROUNDING DISTRICTS.
All who are desirous of witnessing the Extra-
ordinary Performances of M. BLONDIN must
avail themselves of this opportunity of seeing
them in Adelaide, as he will leave shortly for
London, being engaged to appear at the Crystal
Palace, Sydneham, at an early date.   18c

on stilts. Amazing. No wonder he became known as 'The Hero of Niagara'.

From then on his was a household name around the world. He continued to perform his extraordinary feats throughout America and Europe for many years, without ever having even a minor accident or causing injury to others.

With that impressive background one can understand the excitement generated in South Australia when it was announced that the 51-year-old Blondin would be visiting Adelaide and giving one of his amazing performances in the South Parklands on February 6th, 1875 – and what a show it turned out to be.

A canvas enclosure was erected, estimated to hold 15,000 people and the evening performances went on for a week. The area was 'splendidly lit by brilliant and coloured fires and new dazzling magnesium limelight effects'. The beginning of each performance was announced by the report of a gun and the appearance of Blondin dressed in a suit of armour which 'flashed and glittered in the beams of the setting sun'. The talented man astounded his audience by marching across the wire to the

*(from the 'South Australian Register',
3rd February, 1875)*

strands of military music, by dancing, somersaulting, laying on the wire full length, standing on his head, dressing as a French cook and appearing with a stove on his back, from which he calmly sat down half-way across and cooked an omelette, standing on a chair, sitting on the chair, climbing over it and then repeating his famous Niagara trick of walking the distance across the rope with a man on his back. As a finale Blondin dressed in a Polish costume and rode a bicycle across. Needless to say, everyone left quite overwhelmed with wonder at the man's talent and daring.

Proceeds from the final performance were presented to the Mayor of Adelaide for distribution to various charities. The 'Hero of Niagara' lived up to his reputation.

Throughout history genuine class acts, no matter what field, have drawn their imitators and it was no surprise that a spate of 'Australian Blondins' bobbed up all over the place, including Adelaide.

One of the first to display his talents here actually beat M. Blondin to South Australia, he came in 1865. Whoever he was he billed himself as M. Vertelli, the Australian Blondin. Vertelli outdid the real Blondin's later Adelaide exploits by really tempting disaster. He stretched a 100ft wire from one cliff to the other above the waterfall at Waterfall Gully, then a very popular honeymoon hideaway. The wire was simply attached to trees on either side. He walked the wire twice and performed on it in true Blondin style, much to the admiration and trepidation of the huge crowd watching. One slip would have sent Vertelli crashing to the jagged rocks below.

In 1881 another 'Australian Blondin' arrived in Adelaide. This man's real name was James Alexander but the Blondin tag was obviously better for business. Alexander chose the Torrens Lake as the scene for his daring display, just a short distance west of the Morphett Street bridge. The wire stretched across the lake for a distance of 600ft. The crowd drawn by this 'Australian Blondin' totalled about 8,000 so it became a real picnic day by the Torrens and a very profitable one for Alexander. His performance however was a bit tame compared to that of Vertelli and the real Blondin and at one stage he appeared a bit nervous when a slight wind sprang up.

A few years later, in 1888, the South Australian public were given a real treat, a wire-walking performance claimed to be easily the best since the Blondin visit. This time there were two daredevils, Madame Ella Zuila and her daughter Lulu.

Waterfall Gully shortly after the turn of the century.

Forty years earlier the 'Australian Blondin' stretched a 100ft wire from one cliff to the other above the waterfall, at a point close to where this photo was taken. The daredevil acrobat thrilled the admiring audience below with antics copied from the amazing repertoire of the true Blondin, the 'Hero of Niagara'. The master himself visited South Australia in 1875 and performed to mammoth crowds in Adelaide's South Parklands.

(postcard from the private collection of Jenice Chapman)

The site selected was the Adelaide Oval and the South Australian Cricket Association joined in by supplying a magnificent display of fireworks. On the night a crowd of 10,000 jostled into the Oval grounds. Seldom had such a crowd been seen at the Oval. The grounds were illuminated with an ample number of Vauxhall lamps and a special music rotunda, in which the Southern Suburban Band played, was covered in Chinese lanterns. The wire was stretched between platforms and was lit by lanterns at either end. Atmosphere abounded before the performance began.

Madame Zuila and little Lulu matched all the feats of Blondin at Niagara but admittedly weren't faced with certain death had they fallen, there was a safety net in place. Nevertheless, the audience were spellbound by their antics. There was running across the wire, the wheelbarrow push, tricks with a table and chair, a blindfold walk and a pushbike ride. And there was more. A third performer appeared, 'Nyra the Cloud-Flyer'. That brave fellow was hurled from a Roman catapult to a waiting safety net some distance away. What a night at the Adelaide Oval.

The days of Blondin and his imitators have long passed. Their colourful antics at those Adelaide beauty spots are no longer a memory, they happened far too long ago. All the same, it is hard these days to make a visit to Waterfall Gully without half noticing a vision through the mist of one of the Australian Blondins slowly edging his way from one cliff to the other, high above the falls.

9 The Crimean Trophies

I do not like guns, never have, but I admit I can't go past an old cannon in a park or wherever else without stopping, inspecting, wondering and photographing. Well, their days of destruction are done so admiration from a distance of time is permissible, so I tell myself.

Two of my favourites, for there are a pair of them, are really worth inspecting, wondering about and certainly photographing. They are the guns that stand in a threatening manner overlooking the Torrens Parade Ground, off Memorial Drive in the heart of the city. Their appearance marks the pair as very old weapons and that is accentuated by the quaint

One of the two Crimean trophies on guard at the Torrens Parade Ground.

The 1824 cannons arrived in Adelaide in 1859 as a gift from the British Government They were positioned on the hill within the Botanic Garden and remained there for over 20 years. They were then passed on to the military and placed outside the Armoury from where the 'noon-day gun' was fired daily. The cannons were given their third and final Adelaide home, the Torrens Parade Ground, in 1902.

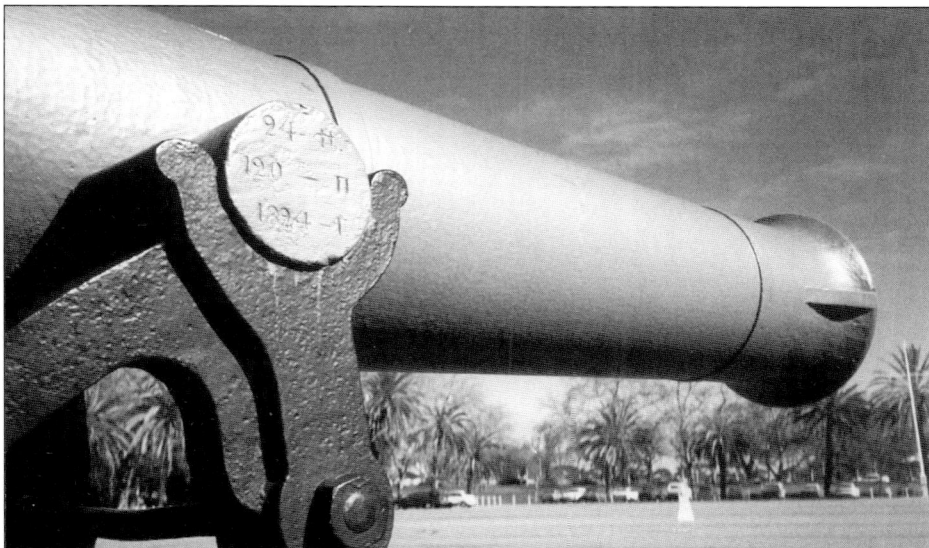

iron garrison carriages supporting them, even though those carriages aren't the originals. When the guns first arrived in Adelaide their carriages were made of timber. Confirmation of the guns' age is obtained when the date on one of the long barrels is read, 1824, twelve years before the first official settlement of South Australia.

The Armoury was within the Police Barracks building off Kintore Avenue.

So, what is the history of these two ancient killing machines? What brought them to Adelaide?

They are in fact Russian guns. The Russian Imperial Eagle can be found on their barrels. They were souvenired at the conclusion of the Crimean War and along with huge quantities of other 'trophies' were shipped to England. Then followed widespread distribution of the former enemy items to all corners of the British Empire, often in pro rata recognition of financial support to a Crimean War Orphans and Widows Relief Fund. The number of Russian guns taken home by the British exceeded one thousand so something had to be done with them. Each of the Australian colonies received two cannons, with the exception of Western Australia. Perhaps their support to mother England's Relief Fund had not been considered satisfactory.

When the cannons arrived in Adelaide in 1859 no decision had been made as to where they would be displayed. The Board of the Botanic Garden saw an opportunity and appealed to Parliament to have them placed in the Garden. At that time the newly established Botanic Garden had very little statuary or other special features and the Crimean trophies would certainly be an attraction. The request was granted and the pair of guns duly mounted on the hill by the eastern wall, adjacent to the Lunatic Asylum. They were, for the record, aimed into the garden and not over the wall.

And there they remained for several years, occasionally being fired as a special salute to someone or something. The most notable such duty was to announce the arrival in Adelaide of Prince Alfred, the Duke of Edinburgh, in 1867.

In the early 1880s the cannons were removed from the Botanic Garden and handed over to the military. It was probably at that time the old wooden carriages were replaced with those of iron. Their new home was outside the Armoury, off Kintore Avenue. The Armoury was built during 1854/55 and first served the Mounted Police who also carried out some military functions. It housed a large cache of arms and was situated in the centre of the building on the southern side of the enclosed quadrangle that served as the Police Parade Ground. Within the same long building, on either side of the Armoury, were quarters for two Inspectors. The remaining space in the southern wing was allocated to orderly rooms and an office. The Crimean guns were placed by the door of the Armoury, aiming towards the passing parade on North Terrace.

There was no permanent military force created in South Australia until 1878 although a local volunteer force was established at the time of the Crimean War. It seems a little strange that the Armoury was not originally favoured ahead of the Botanic Garden for the placement of the guns, however, once they were there, they were used by the military force on a daily basis as part of their training. A 'noon-day gun' was fired every day to both keep the soldiers in practice and to save the general public the worry of relying on the varying times of the Post Office and Town Hall clocks.

Finally, in 1902 their days of usefulness came to an end. The two old cannons were given some much needed renovation and moved to their third South Australian home, at the Torrens Parade Ground. The parade ground and barracks came into being ten years earlier, in 1892, when the South Australian Parliament decided, no doubt against public opinion, to commandeer yet another corner of Colonel Light's Parklands. Following Federation in 1901 the site was taken over by the national defence force. That transfer was made without cost to Canberra and became a contentious issue in 1996 when it was decided the Torrens Parade Ground was no longer needed and the land could be sold.

At the time of writing the fate of the site has still not been decided and the future positioning of the old Crimean trophies remains uncertain.

10   *The Murder of Harry Pearce*

There is a very old cemetery at Walkerville. By the western boundary is a tall monument which, because of its hight, stands out from the rest. The cemetery contains a number of fascinating historical headstones that reveal glimpses of trials and tribulations of South Australia's early days and the tall pillar topped with the shrouded, wreathed urn is one of the most interesting. It tells of high drama that unfolded one day in 1881 down the Coorong.

> *"In memory of*
> *Harry Edmonds Pearce*
> *aged 24 years.*
>
> *A member of the South*
> *Australian Mounted Police*
> *Force, who was cruelly*
> *murdered while escorting*
> *a prisoner near Kingston*
> *on the 16th day of May 1881.*
>
> *Erected by the officers*
> *and his late comrades of*
> *the South Australian Police*
> *Force."*

The story of Harry Pearce's murder actually begins at Wellington with the unlikely scenario of a group of natives being locked up for over-imbibing. Corporal Tom Solly was the policeman at Wellington who had put an end to the prisoners' night of revelry and the following morning gleaned from them the name of the person who had illegally supplied them with the liquor, Robert Johnson. Johnson had been stopping at a wine shop across the river at East Wellington.

Corporal Solly approached Johnson, charged him and told him that a magistrate would hear the case later that day, back across the river at the

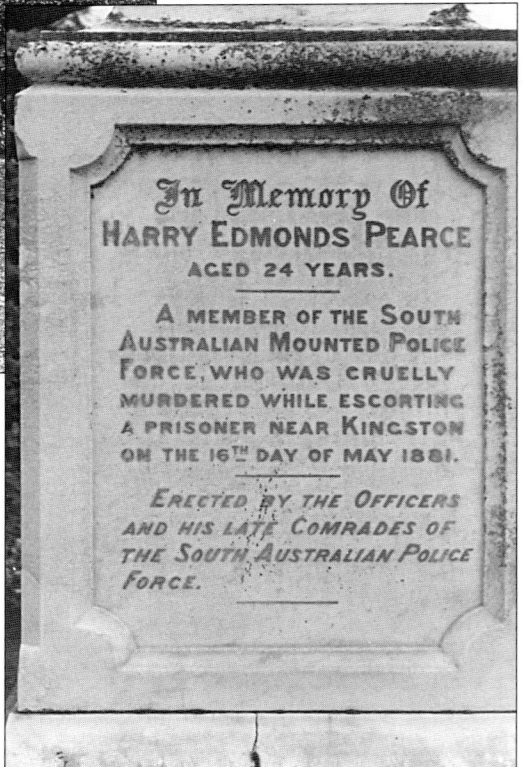

In Memory Of
HARRY EDMONDS PEARCE
AGED 24 YEARS.

A MEMBER OF THE SOUTH
AUSTRALIAN MOUNTED POLICE
FORCE, WHO WAS CRUELLY
MURDERED WHILE ESCORTING
A PRISONER NEAR KINGSTON
ON THE 16TH DAY OF MAY 1881.

ERECTED BY THE OFFICERS
AND HIS LATE COMRADES OF
THE SOUTH AUSTRALIAN POLICE
FORCE.

The memorial in the Walkerville cemetery to murdered Mounted Policeman Harry Pearce.

The murder took place near Kingston in the state's south east but Pearce's family were from Walkerville. His father was the Hon. James Pearce M.L.C. Constable Pearce was given a full police burial.

Wellington Court House. He then returned to the station to make the arrangements, accepting Johnson's word that he would follow within the hour. The magistrate, the policeman and the natives then waited, and waited. Mr. Johnson did not turn up. He had decided to beat a fast retreat and headed south down the Coorong.

Three days later the over-trusting Wellington authorities issued a warrant for the arrest of Robert Johnson. Mounted Constable Dittmar rode with the warrant as far as Meningie and not meeting up with his quarry sent the details of the warrant by telegram further south to the Police Station at Kingston.

By dawn of the following morning Robert Johnson had arrived at Salt Creek, almost halfway between Meningie and Kingston. He was quietly watering his horses by the home of farmer Joseph Walker and when approached by Walker was offered food for his horses and a place to rest for a while. Johnson fed his horses in the barn and took breakfast himself but then declared he would continue on as the police at Wellington were probably after him for supplying drink to the blacks. And on he rode towards Kingston.

The next evening the fugitive arrived at the farm of William and Sarah Smith, just seven miles from Kingston. He knew the Smiths and asked if he could put his horses in the barn and be given a bed for the night himself.

Both requests were granted. Meanwhile, in response to the telegrammed warrant and other information received Mounted Constable Harry Pearce was making arrangements to leave Kingston at 4.15 the next morning in the hope of meeting up with Johnson and making an arrest.

It did not take the young policeman long to carry out his duty for it was just breaking day as he drew level with the Smith farm and noticed extra horses in the barn. He woke the household and enquired if they had someone staying overnight. Without an argument, the supplier of drink gave himself up and agreed to accompany Constable Pearce back into Kingston.

Constable Pearce, like Corporal Solly back at Wellington, was clearly a very trusting person and perhaps did not regard his prisoner as a real criminal. He did not bother to search him nor did he use the handcuffs. He simply agreed that Johnson could ride alongside him and off they went, according to William Smith, on quite friendly terms. Unfortunately for both of them that display of friendship was not to last.

When the two men reached the Kingston four-mile post Johnson stated that he would go no further, dismounted and began to light his pipe. Pearce immediately swung to the ground and ordered him to get back on his horse or he would be handcuffed. Johnson agreed and as Pearce turned to remount he was tackled from behind and slashed across the body with a long knife. A fierce struggle followed, the Constable trying with all his might to relieve Johnson of the knife and at the same time reach for his own revolver. The two rolled on the ground and Pearce received slashes about his hands and then a long, deep, very serious cut across his abdomen. He became faint and was soon overpowered.. The unfortunate over-trusting Constable was relieved of his gun, which was emptied and thrown into the scrub. He was then dragged well off the road and left there to fend for himself. Johnson then turned the policeman's horse adrift and promptly rode away, back towards Meningie.

Two hours later a Kingston farmer, William Dungey, came along the road and was attracted by a handkerchief being waved some distance off. He investigated and found the severely injured, semi-conscious Constable who was able to tell him all that had happened. Contractor Thomas Redman's dray then arrived on the scene and was hailed by Dungey. It was considered unwise to move Pearce because of his hideous stomach wounds so Dungey hurried back into Kingston to get help while Redman's men remained with Harry Pearce.

Others arrived and by the time Sergeant Morris of Kingston reached his colleague there were several men comforting him. No medical help however was available, there was no Doctor in Kingston. The men gently lifted Pearce into a cart and he was slowly taken back into town while Morris took a man with him, Peter Anderson, and hurried off in pursuit of Johnson.

The Sergeant was able to find and follow the fugitive's tracks and had covered about twenty miles when he suddenly caught up with him. Johnson gave no resistance, was searched and charged with the attempted murder of Constable Pearce, escorted back to Kingston and there, in the Police Station, Pearce and Johnson met up with each other again in entirely different circumstances.

Pearce was by then at death's door but was fully conscious and was able to identify Johnson as his attacker. He also confirmed that the knife taken by Sergeant Morris from Johnson's pocket at the time of his arrest was the knife used to cause his injuries. The prisoner's fate was then and there sealed for the following day Constable Harry Pearce died and the charge was altered to that of murder.

Then came confusion as to who Robert Johnson actually was. He claimed that was his name yet in his swag Morris had found several letters addressed to William Nugent. Eventually he admitted he was in fact Nugent and Johnson was simply an alias, that he was a widower, lived in the Gippsland district of Victoria and had a brother John Nugent living at Warrnambool. Brother John was contacted and the prisoner's identity confirmed. It was also established that William Nugent was a regular horse-thief who operated in both colonies.

Harry Pearce was the son of the Hon. James Pearce M.L.C. A family group, father, mother, a sister and a brother arrived in Kingston by the steamer 'Euro' shortly before he died. Dr. Wigg of Adelaide was with them and Dr. Gunning from Naracoorte had arrived sometime earlier but it was too late for the medicos to save him. The family returned to Adelaide with Harry's body and he was given a full police burial at Walkerville.

For his savage crime William Nugent alias Robert Johnson was executed at the Mount Gambier gaol on 18th November, 1881. The fine that would have been imposed on him for supplying liquor to the natives at Wellington would have probably been one pound. His decision to avoid that and make a run for it proved to be a tragic mistake.

The Koolunga Bunyip

The Sturt Reserve at Murray Bridge is a very peaceful and picturesque leisure spot – the big lazy river, a paddlesteamer or two, the excellent view of the differing spans of the old bridge, wonderful trees, birds everywhere, expansive lawns – but what on earth is that terrible roar that upsets the tranquillity every now and then? Drift across to the strange-looking cave structure, place twenty cents in the slot and you will find out. You will have released the fearsome Bertha the bunyip and her equally frightening offspring from the depths of their slime-covered waterhole.

Bunyips have caught the imagination of Australians since the very earliest days of settlement. To our forebears they were quite real. Just about everyone knew someone whose father's workmate, or brother's friend, or friend's grandfather, had actually seen one. The mysterious creature that lived in waterholes and billabongs, ate aborigines, had varying strange physical features and projected a spine-chilling roar through the silent bush in the wee small hours was so real in the minds of the newly arrived Europeans that in the 1820s the Geographical Society of Australia offered to reimburse explorer Hamilton Hume for expenses incurred should he be able to produce evidence of the bunyip's existence.

The majority of sightings over the years centred around the Murrumbidgee district of New South Wales and throughout western Victoria. There was great excitement at Wagga in 1847 when an unusual skull was found. Experts in Sydney later described it as belonging to an animal placed somewhere between a horse and a llama. Numerous theories were put forward, the most widely accepted being that it was the skull of a deformed calf but local natives insisted it was taken from the skeleton of a bunyip that they themselves had trapped and killed.

The first recorded appearance in South Australia came in 1853 when a Mount Gambier farmer spotted a strange creature wallowing in a waterhole on his property. Another twenty years went by however before bunyip-mania really hit this state.

In the 1870s, by the Rocky River on the outskirts of Crystal Brook, a

The fearsome Bertha the bunyip and her equally frightening offspring emerge from the depths of their slime-covered waterhole at the Sturt Reserve, Murray Bridge.

well-placed shanty did a steady trade with local settlers and passing travellers. Close to the shanty was the rather deep Warra Warra waterhole and the shanty keeper promoted widely the existence therein of a resident bunyip. Not only that, there was supposedly an underground channel connecting the waterhole to the sea. A story also circulated that a thirsty bullock team had rushed into the waterhole and promptly disappeared without trace.

The settlers around Crystal Brook became so convinced about the existence of the bunyip that they regularly formed parties to man the banks, ready with rifles to make a killing and so prove to outside doubters that there really was something unique about their Warra Warra waterhole. Unfortunately the nights chosen for the bunyip-kill were always the nights the monster failed to turn up.

Eventually, the Warra Warra bunyip was dismissed as nothing more than a crafty move by the shanty keeper to improve his takings but in 1883 its one time probability once again became fact throughout the district. There were new sightings, not that far away at Koolunga.

Bunyip Park at Koolunga is a reminder that this is where it all happened – where there were numerous sightings of a bunyip during the 1880s. The locals were so determined to prove the existence of the bunyip to the many doubters that they blew up the waterhole with dynamite, hoping, one would imagine, that enough of the unfortunate creature would be left to satisfy the sceptics.

On one bright moonlit Summer's night a bunyip with two of its young were seen in the Broughton River just out of Koolunga. A reporter subsequently visited the town and wrote, 'Ere that I have past little credence to the story of the bunyip but now I am beginning to waver in my opinion as they were seen by several reliable people whose testimony I can well vouch for. There is little doubt that the bunyip is here.'

Certainly there was little doubt in the minds of the Koolunga locals for plans were quickly put in place by several separate groups to capture the beast. One trio, armed to the teeth, positioned themselves at a likely spot by the river and after only a very short time saw, as they later recounted, the bunyip stealthily emerge from the water and come straight towards them. The nerves of the heroes broke and they bolted without firing a shot. Other groups reported seeing the bunyip that same evening and almost every other evening for a whole week. Needless to say, bunyip hysteria raged through Koolunga.

The next move was quite dramatic. An afternoon attempt was made to blow up the monster, hoping, one would imagine, that if successful enough of the unfortunate bunyip would be left to prove its existence to the odd sceptic. A procession of buggies and horsemen arrived at the favoured spot on the river and about twenty men began preparing charges of dynamite. Then came the big moment. A huge explosion. Water everywhere. Dogs yapping with excitement. Breathless anticipation from the picnicking onlookers. Something was floating on the surface. Men with rifles at the ready. And what a let-down, subsequent examination revealed that the object was nothing more than a jumble of reeds and mud disturbed by the explosion.

No doubt that evening the licensee of the Koolunga Hotel, like his counterpart the shanty keeper of Crystal Brook, did a roaring trade over the bar as his disappointed patrons planned their next move. And even to this day, if you visit Koolunga, you will learn that the bunyip is still there and is seen from time to time by reliable locals although recent past attempts to catch him have failed for various reasons. Perhaps come back on the next moonlit night!

12 *The Type Orchard at Mylor*

The 'Type Orchard', now what type of orchard could that be? The one at Mylor, in the Adelaide Hills, was opened in 1899. Its purpose was to test all available varieties of all available fruit trees, to enable growers to identify their varieties and obtain grafts true to name and to provide a base for various experiments that could be beneficial to the burgeoning South Australian fruit growing industry. The orchard covered approximately 17 acres and contained over 6500 trees, bushes and vines. The very costly but seemingly worthwhile project was sponsored by the Government and carried out by the Adelaide Botanic Garden.

The project was however a bit of a fizzer, it did not fulfil expectations. The soil proved to be unsuitable for many trees, the winters too severe and the site was considered customer unfriendly, major factors that should have been apparent before the huge amounts of public money were spent on this fruit dream that failed to come to fruition. By 1907 the transfer of many trees to other locations had commenced.

The proposal to create the Type Orchard was first considered by Government in 1897. Why the Mylor site was selected is a bit of a puzzle. It was land by the banks of the Onkaparinga River that had formerly been set aside as an aboriginal reserve. It was decided upon when the initial favoured location, the old Exhibition Ground by Frome Road, was chosen for other purposes.

The Gardens management must have been fully aware of the standard of the soil, described afterwards as being of 'poor and hungry character, very freely interspersed with soft, crumbly sandstone and below the average quality of hills land'. A justifying argument put forward by the Commissioner of Crown Lands, that they wanted to test the poorest hills land for apples and pears, would have failed to impress those who felt public money should be directed in more urgent social directions. And those who thought the orchard too inaccessible were told that was a plus factor as it was a safeguard against disease and anyone really interested should be capable of making the journey to Mylor.

When first laid out, the orchard was a wonderful showpiece. Initially the 17 acres of fairly steep hillside had to be cleared and then suitably surrounded with a 'hare-proof' fence. The 5300 trees and 1500 small fruits, the majority of which had been imported from European nurseries, were meticulously planted exactly 12ft from each other. Each tree was in the centre of a circle of six. A visitor looking in any direction would be looking down a straight line of trees, a very pleasing effect. Every tree, bush and vine had its zinc label affixed to a jarrah stake showing all the necessary information about that particular fruit. The site may have been customer unfriendly but the display was perfect.

The orchard was made up of apples, pears, quinces, medlars, plums, persimmons, almonds, chestnuts, walnuts, peaches, nectarines, apricots, cherries, citrus, figs, mulberries, filbert nuts, olives, currants, gooseberries, raspberries, blackberries, strawberries and grapevines. The orchard's collection was believed to be the largest in the southern hemisphere at the time and larger than any in America as well.

A number of permanent buildings were built to service the orchard and house the staff. They included two cottages, stables, work sheds, store

One of the two surviving mulberry trees of the 1899 Type Orchard at Mylor. Over 6,500 various fruit trees, bushes and vines were planted in an overly ambitious project by the Government. Most were transferred to a more suitable location in 1907.

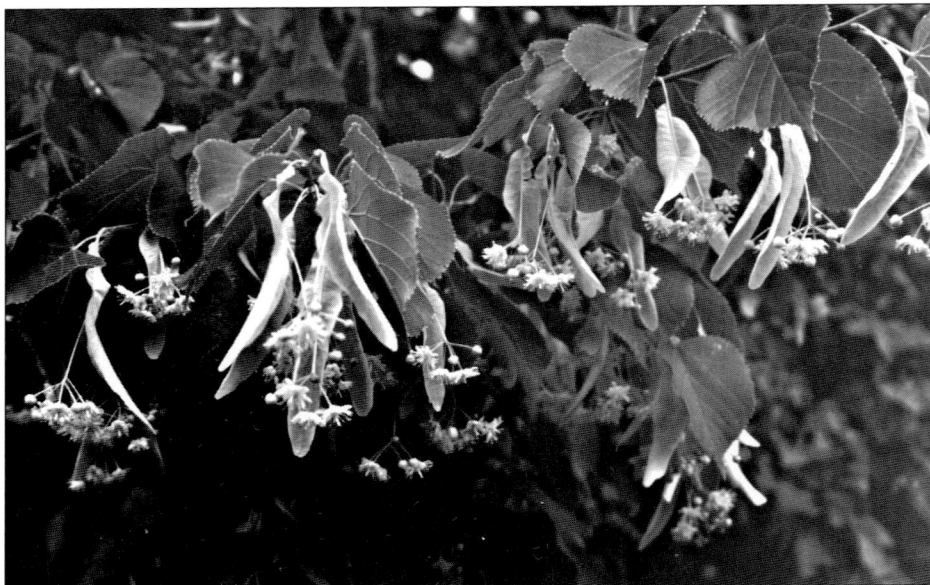

The small fragrant yellowish blossom of the Linden tree at Mylor, one of the few survivors from when the Mylor Type Orchard became an arboretum for shade trees, timber trees and ornamental trees in 1911.

sheds and other outbuildings. Water was pumped from the Onkaparinga to the brow of the hill and from there re-diverted to all parts of the orchard. Permanent Botanic Garden staff were assigned to this interesting outstation and a good deal of local casual labour was also used. It certainly was an expensive undertaking.

The orchard was officially opened in November 1899 and by then the total expenditure was already reaching towards two thousand pounds. The Board of the Botanic Garden decided to celebrate the opening by entertaining themselves, along with the Premier and other Government leaders, at the site – hang the expense.

So, on that special day, the 10th November 1899, a very important group of 20 dignitaries assembled at the Adelaide Railway Station and left town by the 10.30 am train for Aldgate. At least they did not requisition a special train. The V.I.Ps were met at the Aldgate Station by vehicles to convey them through the hills to Mylor. Neatly packed away in one of the vehicles was a lavish lunch prepared by Mrs. Watts of the Aldgate Hotel, cigars and liquid refreshments included.

Following the mandatory inspection of the vast orchard, lunch was served in the main cottage, and following lunch the speeches commenced. For a few entertaining hours, Government members and Gardens representatives congratulated each other. If anyone present had lurking doubts about the correctness of the project or the excellence of the work carried out to date then those doubts would have been completely eliminated by the time the happy fellows were returned safely to the Aldgate Hotel. Mrs. Watts added considerably to her day's profits by the time her distinguished guests boarded the evening train for Adelaide.

It must have been only a few short years following this confident beginning that the Director of the Botanic Garden, Dr. Holtze, would have realised that all was not well. Eight years went by before he was able to convince the Board, and in turn the Government, that a move should be made. The numerous varieties of fruit trees that had proved unsuitable for the conditions were transferred to Hackney, to the newly established 'Demonstration and Experimental Orchard', which was controlled by the State Agricultural Department.

Yet another move became necessary shortly after when the Hackney land was handed on to the Municipal Tramways Trust. The trees were given their third home, this time at Blackwood, where another experimental orchard was established.

In 1911 the Mylor orchard was re-developed as an arboretum. It became a testing ground for shade trees, timber trees and ornamental trees as well as a nursery for supplying public parks and gardens. Because a spattering of suitable-to-the-location fruit trees survived the cull it became known as the Mylor Type Orchard and Arboretum.

All that remains today of the ambitious project are remnants of some of the old buildings and just a few gnarled old trees, including two mulberries and a splendid Linden tree. The vast area sweeping down to the river is now practically all bare, open land.

13 *Once I Wasn't, Then I Was, Now I Ain't Again*

That down to earth summary of life and death apparently comes from a tombstone in an American wild west 'Boot Hill'. I much prefer the more colourful and quizzical epitaphs from old English churchyards. Fortunately the latter have been adopted here in South Australia. One I particularly like is -

"Sinners all as you pass by,
As you are now so once was I,
As I am now so you will be,
Prepare thyself to follow me ...'

I am never sure whether that old chestnut is placed on a headstone to chill or to amuse. I first read it in the historic cemetery of St. John's, at Parramatta, in New South Wales, above a grave that dated back almost 200 years. I have since found reference to it appearing on much older headstones in English churchyards and in recent times came across it in a lonely South Australian country cemetery. Is the permanent placement of such a ditty the result of fore-planning by people with a quirky sense of humour or of similarly endowed relatives after the event? If the latter, the former would certainly be in no position to object.

There are scores of such delightful epitaphs to be read in South Australian graveyards. Burial grounds are not just places to visit during times of traumatic bereavement, or follow-up remembrance. They are also places for learning, for relaxation and even enjoyment. A student can often learn more of local history and of past local identities in cemeteries than in text books. The peaceful surroundings are certainly relaxing and the humour and wisdom of scribes from the past can keep one entertained for hours.

It is not only clever or meaningful inscriptions that set you wondering. Often a headstone itself is out of the ordinary, possibly shaped to

At Jamestown is the ultimate headstone. The actual quarry stone that killed two men, William Vince and Henri Nottebaum, adorns their grave in the local cemetery. The accident occurred in 1878.

represent a particular profession, or happening, or positioned in an unusual way, or constructed of something different.

One that really stops you in your tracks, as indeed it did to the gentlemen resting below, can be found at Jamestown, in the state's mid north. When first sighted it looks uncannily like a loaf of bread but on closer inspection you read the awful inscription – "killed by this stone". The huge rock above the dual grave was actually one of several that fell during a quarrying accident which resulted in the deaths in 1878 of William Vince and Henri Nottebaum.

Other scenes of accidental deaths are sometimes memorialised by carved likenesses of the locations, such as that of a lighthouse on a headstone in the Cheltenham cemetery, marking the grave of Harry Franson. Harry was accidentally killed at the Wonga Shoal Lighthouse, off Semaphore, in 1912. The touching verse on the stone, apparently the thoughts of his widow, add to the sadness of the moment when reading this headstone -

"I never thought when I wished him goodbye,
I left him alone at the lighthouse to die ..."

Then there are several profession, or occupational headstones, such as the pink marble bass drum in the West Terrace cemetery. This prominent memorial tells passers-by that Leonard Massey, who died in 1939, was a drummer in John Martin's orchestra. There are in fact many 'musical' headstones around the state. An imaginative cartoonist or story-teller could very well compose eerie pieces about after dark groups entertaining their silent neighbours – there are plenty of harps to be found in South Australian graveyards, plus the odd violin, a trumpet or two, even a guitar and a few keyboards.

At Moorlands we find the 'horseman's' grave, at Mount Burr the 'bullocky's' and at Stenhouse Bay the 'seaman's'. The horseman's grave at Moorlands appears to be a memorial to horsemen generally, although perhaps an unknown pioneer could actually be buried there. The smartening up of the grave and the setting of a plaque became a Jubilee project in 1986. On top of the headstone sit a pair of horseshoes.

The bullocky's grave at Mount Burr is that of 16-year-old Dugald Steele who was killed by a bull and buried on the spot in 1850. Dugald arrived in the district, along with his parents, the year before and the family settled close by at Mt. Muirhead Station. Another sad headstone is in the vicinity, traveller Ellen Hogarth's. Ellen died in her dray when travelling from Mount Barker to Mount Gambier in 1862.

The seaman's grave at Stenhouse Bay belongs to Dao Thanh, bosun on the S.S. 'Notue' in 1940. Dao Thanh had been struck by a swinging bag of coal as the ship was approaching Stenhouse Bay and the coal cargo was being re-positioned to make way for a load of gypsum. His neck was broken and he died instantly. Dao was a Buddhist, a religion that forbade burial at sea so after the 'Notue' berthed, the body of the unfortunate bosun was buried high on the cliff above the bay.

Up in the Flinders Ranges, within the historic Beltana cemetery, we find a Sunday School teacher being remembered. A solitary metal hand holding a bible is positioned on top of a hoop of iron above the gateway to the enclosure housing the memorial to Anna Doig, who died in 1894.

The unique embellishment to Anna's gravesite immediately catches the eye when first entering this fascinating old cemetery. The inscription on the headstone was placed there by the teachers and scholars of the Beltana Sunday School.

Mrs. Doig's husband was the local blacksmith and no doubt it was he who fashioned the hand and bible. Peter Doig's blacksmith premises first adjoined and then took over the original Beltana Court House, which later became the Smith of Dunesk Mission. It was from there that Flynn of the Inland, the Rev. John Flynn, founded the Australian Inland Mission which led to the establishment of the world-famous Flying Doctor Service.

Another eye-catcher is in the Church of England cemetery at Clare, a small, simple stone announcing the resting place of Martha Forbes, 'Old

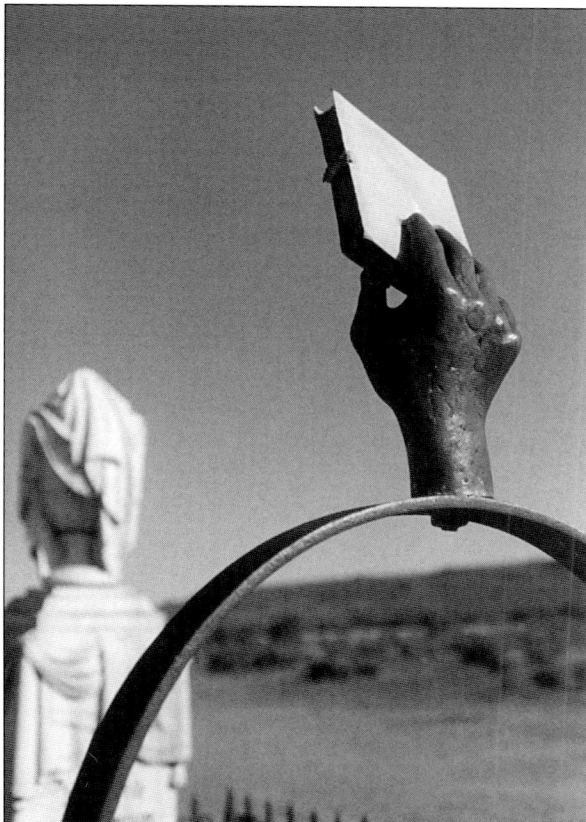

At Beltana, a metal hand holding a bible is positioned above the gateway to the enclosure housing the grave of Sunday School teacher Anna Doig, who died in 1894.

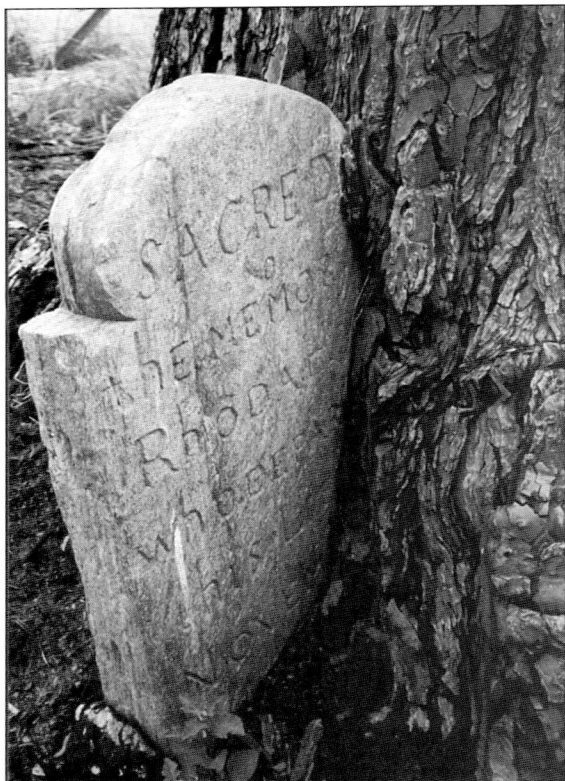

A pine tree was planted over the grave of Rhoda Hunt, who died at Kersbrook in 1865. As the tree grew it began swallowing Rhoda's headstone, so much so that today part of the inscription is lost.

Martha', who died in 1895. Old Martha was a long-time town identity who lived alone in her Gleeson Street cottage. She suffered from a weak spine and shuffled around the streets of Clare bent almost double. The much loved little old lady died in her well-kept garden, supposedly from suffocation after falling face down and being unable to move. The short epitaph on the small stone reads, 'Thou art loosed from thine infirmity'. At least some thoughtful and admiring people saw fit to make sure Old Martha was remembered.

Back to occupational headstones. The most prominent grave site in all of South Australia is marked by a tall marble column and at the peak of the column sits a carved theodolite, telling the world that a surveyor is buried below. That surveyor of course is Colonel Light. The city founder is indeed buried beneath his monument, in the centre of Light Square.

A curious fact of history is that within the Colonel's coffin there is a plaque confirming that he was Adelaide's founder, its positioning being one of his final requests. We will of course have to take the word of others on that, it would be a little difficult to prove.

There are two headstones associated with trees that are certainly fascinating, one at Lobethal and one at Kersbrook. The Lobethal stone embraces two adjoining graves and memorialises an engaged couple, Maria and Carl, who died in 1877. A week prior to their planned marriage Maria died and Carl followed within the month, supposedly of a broken heart. Two pine trees were planted above the graves and over the years the trees have grown as one. From a distance there appears to be only one tree and that has become known locally as 'The Lovers' Tree'.

A pine tree was also planted over the Kersbrook grave, that of Rhoda Hunt, who died in 1865. As the tree grew its trunk swallowed up Rhoda's headstone, so much so that today only portion of the inscription can be read. In recent times the large old tree has been cut down but fortunately only to a level just above the trapped headstone. As a result, both stone and stump now present a very sad picture.

The memorials to Maggie, Squeakie and Wow at Marble Hill – or are they memorials to the eccentricity of Lady Barclay-Harvey?

Three of the most surprising headstones in South Australia are to be found at Marble Hill, within the haunting ruins of the burnt-out vice-regal residence which was decimated by the bush fires of 1955. The small, neat stones are close together, in formation, with only a tiny grave space surrounding them. On first sighting their size and positioning are quite puzzling but all becomes clear when the inscriptions are read. The stones record the burials of Maggie, Squeakie and Wow, pet dogs of Lady Muriel Barclay-Harvey.

Lady Muriel was the wife of Sir Malcolm Barclay-Harvey, State Governor from 1939 to 1944. She brought to South Australia a number of pet dogs. Some of them died at Marble Hill and were buried in the grounds of the mansion, each with its own personal headstone. For the record, Maggie was a black Labrador, Squeakie was a West Highland terrier and Wow was a Welsh corgi. The dogs of Marble Hill will be remembered while the identity of the pioneer horseman of Moorlands will forever remain a mystery.

There are literally hundreds of such interesting stories to be unearthed, sorry, discovered in South Australia's graveyards.

14   *The Mayoral Chairs*

Two unrelated maritime disasters, 48 years apart, one in New Zealand waters and the other in South Australia's Spencer Gulf, have an unusual common sequel. Salvaged timbers from each wreck were used to create the Mayoral chairs for two South Australian regional councils.

The ship lost off the coast of New Zealand was none other than the 'Buffalo', the vessel on which South Australia's first Governor, Captain John Hindmarsh, arrived. It ran aground in Mercury Bay in July 1840. The other was the barque 'Saturn' which caught fire in the Port Pirie harbour in January 1888 after taking on 14,000 bushels of wheat. The first of the chairs to be built came from the retrieved timbers of the 'Saturn' and was presented to the Port Pirie Council. That occurred shortly after the barque's 1888 burning and quite possibly prompted the creation of the 'Buffalo' chair for the Glenelg Council eleven years later.

The 'Saturn' was a 10-year-

The Port Pirie Mayoral chair was built from timbers salvaged from the German barque 'Saturn' which was destroyed by fire in the Port Pirie harbour in 1888. A local German, Theo Kneese, crafted the chair as a permanent memorial to a ship from his homeland that came to grief at his adopted home.

(Photograph taken with permission of Port Pirie Regional Council)

old German ship and the wheat cargo was destined for the United Kingdom. On the night of 6th January she was sitting at anchorage waiting for the necessary clearance papers. Captain Maas, his wife and three children were asleep in the main cabin and around midnight one of his daughters awoke to suffocating smoke. She gave the alarm and the family and crew all narrowly escaped from certain death for the fire was well established and spreading rapidly through the wooden ship.

The master of the tug 'Nelcebee' was first to notice the burning vessel and sounded the alarm through sending up rockets and blowing the tug's steam whistle. The 'Copsfield' was anchored nearby and immediately sent boats to rescue the panic-stricken people. The tug then hitched on to the doomed ship and pushed her at full speed onto Cockle Spit, about two miles distant. There was nothing that could be done to save the 'Saturn'. The fire continued to burn and the spectacle became a real attraction for the residents of Port Pirie. Throughout the following afternoon the 'Nelcebee' took about 180 sightseers to view the smouldering wreck.

Captain Maas was in a desperate situation. He was part owner of the 'Saturn' and the ship was only partly insured. He and his family had lost everything, they had no money and only the clothes they were wearing. Maas contacted, by telegram, the German Consul in Adelaide and requested immediate assistance. The Consul personally attended the subsequent inquest at Port Pirie and gave the necessary help to the Maas family.

The remains of the 'Saturn' were auctioned but there was really little to salvage. Total proceeds amounted to less than fifty pounds. The Consul declared that the full amount should be passed on to the Captain of the 'Nelcebee'. Enough timber was however retrieved for one special project. Theo Kneese, a local German, was an accomplished carpenter and he created a lasting memorial to the ship from his homeland that had come to grief at his adopted home. Kneese built a fine chair from the scraps and presented it to the town of Port Pirie to be used as the Mayoral chair. The chair has now been in constant use for over a century and is in fine condition.

South Australia's other disaster-born Mayoral chair was built many years after its host ship was lost. The 'Buffalo' came to grief in 1840, the Glenelg Mayoral chair was not created until 1899.

South Australia's most famous historically significant ship was built in Calcutta in 1813 and was first named the 'Hindustan'. She was later

The Glenelg Mayoral chair was built in 1899 from timber retrieved from the remains of the 'Buffalo', which was wrecked in New Zealand waters in 1840.

(Photographs taken with permission of City of Holdfast Bay)

Beneath the seat of the Glenelg Mayoral chair are two pieces of untreated, unworked teak direct from the 'Buffalo' wreck, a physical tie to the legendary ship that so strongly features in South Australia's history.

purchased by the Royal Navy who gave her the name change. The 'Buffalo' was used for several purposes both before and after bringing our first Governor to Holdfast Bay in 1836. Her first visit to Australia was in 1833 as a convict ship, transporting 180 female prisoners to Sydney, two of whom died on the voyage. The return journey was made via New Zealand with a load of kauri timber.

Following the 1836 South Australian assignment the 'Buffalo' worked mainly between New South Wales and New Zealand but also managed another return trip to England and then on to Quebec to bring more prisoners down to Hobart. From Van Diemen's Land she returned again to New Zealand for more kauri timber and that was to be her final voyage. It was there on July 28th, 1840, at Mercury Bay on the east coast, that disaster struck.

The 'Buffalo' lay at anchor while several of her crew were up the Whitianga River collecting kauri spurs. At the onset of a fierce storm the Captain attempted to take shelter by entering the river but ran onto rocks. The ship slewed sideways and in the violent winds and current became completely unmanageable, ending up stranded on the beach. The buffeting was so severe that a man and a boy lost their lives during the drama.

Within a short time the 'Buffalo' had completely broken up. The Admiralty eventually sold her to local salvagers and many unsuccessful attempts were made to retrieve what was left. A move was even made to burn some of the timber so as to release various copper fittings but that failed as well. Odd relics were taken by locals but generally the remains of the 'Buffalo' stayed where they were on the newly named Buffalo Beach.

Almost 60 years later, in 1898, the ribs were still visible. An Adelaide visitor, Mr. R. J. Rigaud, was shown the wreck and brought news of its existence to South Australians through a letter to the press. The Mayor of Glenelg, Henry Yorke Sparks immediately became interested and began negotiations to retrieve whatever relics were available and possibly some timber as well. He would have been aware of the Port Pirie Mayoral chair and very likely the idea of a Glenelg chair from 'Buffalo' timber came to him at that time.

Mr. Sparks was successful and some timber was obtained. Adelaide architect G. K. Soward was privately commissioned to design a new Mayoral chair and the carriage builders at the St. Leonards Railway Workshops were given the job of constructing it. The resulting 7ft. high unique item of furniture was subsequently presented to the Council by its Mayor and like the earlier built Port Pirie chair is still in good condition and in regular use.

The Glenelg Mayoral chair has an added feature. Beneath the well-padded seat are attached two pieces of untreated, unworked teak direct from the 'Buffalo' wreck. They show clearly the condition of the timber as it was received in 1898 and provide a physical tie to the legendary ship that so strongly features in South Australia's history.

A strange occurrence in 1960 brought the 'Buffalo' once again into public attention. An earthquake in far away Chile sent tidal waves around the Pacific and a sudden surge followed by a retraction of the waters in Mercury Bay exposed for a short time the 'Buffalo's' keel. A new search for relics began and a bulldozer was even used to try to drag the keel to dry land but the normal tides quickly returned and the treasure hunt ended with very little success.

15 *The Black Death*

"Ah-choo! Ah-choo! And we all fall down" – the finishing words and actions of the innocent game we all remember from our childhood, "Ring-A-Ring O'Roses". How strange it is that those final words, chanted by generation after generation of children around the world, actually refer to dying. "Ring-A-Ring O'Roses" had its origin in the middle ages as a gruesome parody on the horrors of the Great Plague. A circle of rose-coloured spots was one of the first signs, various herbs were worn as a conceived protection against the scourge and sneezing was recognised as a warning that death was on its way.

The plague, known as 'The Black Death', first made its awesome appearance in the British Isles around the year 1350, when it was estimated that a third of the population died. The City of London experienced hideous outbreaks in the mid 1600s when somewhere between 70,000 and 100,000 people lost their lives. Old illustrations abound of evil-looking characters pulling their death carts around London alleyways as they call "bring out your dead". A horrible time in English history.

In modern times, control of the population of the plague-carrying black rat, along with dramatically improved hygienic practices, have seen the end of the plague as an epidemic killer but cases still do occur. When that happens, panic always sets in.

So, imagine the excitement around Port Adelaide on the morning of 7th April, 1909, when an official announcement was made through the Central Board of Health that a carter who had been working on the wharves had just died of the plague. The thirty-year-old man had been employed by the carriers Rofe & Co. offloading goods from the steamer 'Carpentaria', which had recently arrived from Newcastle. He became ill only three days before and died just five minutes after being admitted to Mrs. Fisher's Private Hospital in Buller Terrace, Alberton. In the same announcement came the news that a second man was suffering from the plague and was quarantined, along with his wife and child, in his home in Leadenhall Street. He was a wharf labourer who had been working on

Leadenhall Street at Port Adelaide is typical of tidy suburban streets all over the metropolitan area – but not so in 1909. That was the year when the dreaded bubonic plague hit Port Adelaide and two cases were reported from different houses in this street.

There were four deaths at the Port over a few weeks and locals became panic stricken as the Black Death was visiting them only a few years after a devastating epidemic at Johannesburg had taken 82 lives. Health authorities acted quickly and decisively at Port Adelaide, even to the extent of completely demolishing some houses.

the steamer 'Grantala' at Commercial Wharf, adjacent to the 'Carpentaria's' berth at No. 1 Quay.

The first victim lived in Torrens Road at Alberton along with several members of his family. As well as his wife and daughter, both of his parents and three brothers also shared the house. They, like the second man and his wife and child, were isolated in their home. Two policemen were assigned to each place, one at the front and one at the rear.

On the day of the alarming announcement, news reached Adelaide from Sydney that a young man there had also died of the plague and another suffering from it had been admitted to hospital. Where was the source? Was it the 'Carpentaria'? Was it the 'Grantala'? Could it be one of the many other ships currently berthed at Port Adelaide? Speculation was rife.

The body of the Torrens Road man had been wrapped in a shroud soaked in a strong formalin solution, placed in a coffin and removed immediately to a shed within the Cheltenham cemetery. While the grave was being dug, the shed was tightly guarded and final tests were made on the body. Then, without further delay the poor man was buried. The only people permitted to be present were the two Doctors who had been in charge of matters, the curator of the cemetery, the undertaker and the gravedigger. Precautions were at a very high level.

Following the burial the Board of Health attempted to calm the frightened people of Port Adelaide by issuing the statement – "There is no more cause for alarm than in an ordinary outbreak of typhoid". It is hard to believe that would have provided much reassurance, particularly with newspaper reports reminding everyone that 82 deaths had occurred from the plague in Johannesburg only 5 years back.

The second victim and his family were taken to isolation on Torrens Island. His condition did not alter much during the next few days and the Doctors declared that they expected him to recover. The ships and wharves were systematically inspected. Only an odd rat or two were found and disposed of and at the same time great effort was made to quickly clean up rubbish piles lying about the wharves. All people who had contact with either man leading up to April 7th were disinfected and were reporting daily to the medical office. No further cases had been announced and everyone began to feel a little easier – until another bombshell on April 11th. Word quickly spread that an 18-year-old, who lived with his parents in Cannon Street at the Port, had died in the Adelaide Hospital, probably of the plague.

The lad had taken ill the week before and admitted to the Adelaide Hospital as a supposed case of typhoid fever. Doctors shortly afterwards suspected plague and more stringent isolation was adopted. He died the following morning and the presence of the hideous disease was not confirmed until tests taken after death. Victim number 3 had been employed as a clerk in Brown's coal company office at Port Adelaide.

A second wave of panic and precautions began and the young man's parents joined the others on Torrens Island. It would be difficult now to reassure the residents of Port Adelaide that the threat had passed. And their fears were justified. On April 20th came the news that a seaman on the ketch 'Victor', bound from Port Adelaide to Port Broughton, had become ill, was landed at Edithburgh and brought back to the Casualty Hospital at Port Adelaide. The seaman showed symptoms of the plague. The unfortunate man died within two days and following tests taken it was revealed that it was indeed the plague that had brought about his death.

It was now admitted that the disease had established a hold at Port Adelaide but the source could not be found. Blame was apportioned, without evidence, to incoming ships from the eastern states. It was an alarming situation. All the authorities could do was to continue with their inspections and clean-ups and hope that the general public were taking notice of the regular warnings being put out about the disastrous results that could come from filth and vermin left unattended about their homes.

More and more rats were being trapped and examined for fleas for it was the fleas they carried that actually transmitted the plague bacillus. Success came on April 26th, when two rats taken from a house on North Parade tested positive. The property was owned by the South Australian Company and used as a livery stable. An ensuing search brought to light a dead cat and a number of dead rats, all believed victims of the disease. The house was immediately vacated and demolished and at the conclusion of the demolition the open land was thoroughly cleared and cleaned.

This dramatic action accelerated the search, examination and destruction of rats while the Port's horrible nightmare continued. Yet another plague death was suddenly announced, that of a 57-year-old Port Adelaide fisherman. He, like the young clerk, died in the Adelaide Hospital.

Victim number 5 was a bachelor and boarded with a family in Leadenhall Street. During the three weeks leading up to his death he had been working on both the ketch 'Trix' and the fishing cutter 'Renown' as well as generally hanging around the pubs at Port Adelaide. No-one at the Port was now feeling safe. It was revealed that the two who had been conveyed to Adelaide for admission to the Adelaide Hospital had travelled in the luggage van of the suburban train so train travellers on that line also began to worry. The body of the last to die was cremated and all the then too familiar disinfecting procedures were carried out on people and places.

The rat crusade went on as did the rubbish clean-up and the residents of Port Adelaide waited for more disastrous announcements – but no more came. Their worst fears did not eventuate. There was to be no widespread catastrophe as occurred at Johannesburg.

The real-life version of "Ring-A-Ring O'Roses" being played out at the Port had come to an end. Four players had fallen down while one survived – he was the winner. How the game commenced was never accurately established.

16 *All Different ... But the Smoke Goes up the Chimney Just the Same*

There is something about a disused kiln that will often attract and puzzle a passer-by. What could that strange looking building have been used for? What on earth is it?

Kilns come in all shapes and sizes. They burn, bake or dry all sorts of products or produce of numerous industries and there are forlorn ruins of several around South Australia reminding us of different, long-forgotten enterprises. There are of course many currently in use but it is the old ones, those that tell us something of the past, that are the most interesting.

One such monument to the struggles of yesteryear can be found in suburban Trinity Gardens, in Koster Park, between Ashbrook and Avenmore Avenues. This large, strange structure looks more like an overweight minaret from an ancient mosque, or perhaps a European folly of some sort. It stands alone in the middle of the park and to the uninitiated it could be anything. It certainly raises interest when seen for the first time.

The kiln is a relic of Koster's pottery which produced a wide range of pots and pans, jars and jugs, barrels, bottles and bowls and all things pottery over a period of 90 years, from the late 1800s right through to 1977. It began as a brickworks about 1880 but soon after became a specialist pottery. The necessary clay was originally found locally but supply became a problem and thereafter was brought down by rail from north of Port Augusta.

When the business closed down in 1977 the council purchased the land and buildings and demolished everything except the attractive old kiln. They then created Koster Park, much to the pleasure of nearby residents.

From Trinity Gardens we head to the hills, to Lobethal, and there on

The kiln at Trinity Gardens was once part of Koster's Pottery, which stood on the site for a period of 90 years.

Post Office Road we find a hop kiln. Once again, on first sighting it is hard to know just what the building represents for it really appears to be a jumble of afterthoughts of stone, brick and galvanised iron with a little ladder leading to a little loft. It is a romantic sort of a building. It actually replaced an earlier hop kiln on the property, which burnt down, but still dates back to around the year 1900. It is claimed to be the only intact hop kiln in South Australia, although admittedly it is used these days as a barn.

Hop growing never really flourished in South Australia. The plant so necessary in the brewing of beer was much more suited to the constantly colder climate of Tasmania, which became the main centre of the industry in Australia. Plantations in South Australia were confined to sections of the Adelaide Hills and to the Mount Gambier district and were worked mainly between the 1870s and the very early 1900s.

Not far from Lobethal is Carey Gully and there on Nicol's Road we

The well preserved kiln at the abandoned Talisker mine was used to make fire-bricks for the furnaces and flues. Silver-lead ore was mined at the Talisker, which is within the Deep Creek Conservation Park near Cape Jervis.

find another kind of kiln, one once used for drying tobacco. This tall stone structure with the attractive quoins and hipped roof is quite imposing and does not look at all like the traditional tobacco kiln.

The tobacco industry in South Australia was a little like that of hop growing. Only limited attempts were made to establish it because the plant proved unsuitable to local soils and conditions other than in small pockets of the Adelaide Hills. Even so, small tobacco plantations were persevered with from the 1890s through to the 1930s.

One of the very earliest moves to establish a tobacco industry in South Australia was made in 1850. Governor Henry Young brought seed into the colony from Havana and distributed it liberally to potential growers. The trial was virtually a complete failure, the quality of the seed being blamed.

From the hills we head south to the tip of the Fleurieu Peninsula, to the old abandoned Talisker mine near Cape Jervis. The well preserved kiln we find there is hidden away in the undergrowth on the eastern side of the vast complex of ruins. It was used to make fire-bricks for the various furnaces and flues. This kiln could be described as cute and compact yet it also has the forbidding appearance of a pre-historic tomb. It is quite different to those at Trinity Gardens, Lobethal and Carey Gully.

Work to mine the outcrop of silver-lead ore commenced at the Talisker in 1862. By 1865 a treatment and smelting works had been erected, a main shaft had been sunk, an enginehouse and furnaces built. The main shaft went down for 80m. In 1867 a stamp battery was installed and two years later the little kiln was built. By then the main shaft had been extended further down to 132m and fifty men were employed at the mine. It was an over-ambitious undertaking for the following year the mine closed due to water problems, lack of finance and the general low grade of the ore.

The next kiln we visit is across on the eastern side of Yorke Peninsula. This is the biggest of the lot and is actually dug into the cliffs. It is a lime kiln, built between 1900 and 1910 and from the sea looks more like the rampart of a ruined castle than a simple kiln used for the burning of lime.

The production of lime was once a very important industry on Yorke Peninsula and this monster was just one of several kilns along the coastline. It is situated above the Wool Bay jetty from where the lime was easily loaded and shipped across the Gulf to its ready market in Adelaide, to be used as building mortar.

It is wonderful to see these five quite different kilns in such good condition and being well looked after. Each is an important physical reminder of its own particular industry or enterprise.

This old lime kiln looks more like a rampart of an ancient castle. It can be found at Wool Bay, on Yorke Peninsula. The kiln is dug into the cliffs above the jetty from where the lime was easily loaded and shipped across the gulf to Adelaide, to be used as building mortar.

17 *The Offshore Reformatory*

The Largs Pier Hotel was built in 1882. The three-storeyed bluestone building with its numerous stuccoed arches around the verandahs on each level was immediately hailed as one of the colony's grandest structures. It must have presented an impressive and welcoming sight to arriving immigrants, the majority of whom were in those days first setting foot in South Australia on the Largs pier. Outer Harbour was not completed until 1908.

Many newcomers would have spent time on the first day in their new land in the civilised comfort of the majestic hotel and no doubt some would have relaxed on one of the upstairs verandahs, gazing out to sea and feeling very relieved indeed that their long journey had ended safely. In doing so, something would certainly have caught their attention. Well within view was moored a puzzling old hulk, and it seemed to be inhabited. Pictures would come to mind of prison hulks from an earlier age back in their home country, but that couldn't be here in South Australia, or could it?

The hulk in question was all that remained of the formerly famous immigrant ship 'Fitzjames', built in North America in 1852. The 'Fitzjames' made several voyages between England and Australia. The first to Melbourne, in 1854, was marred by a seaman being washed overboard while during her first and only to Adelaide, less than two years later, a seaman fell into the sea from the topsail and rescue attempts failed. On that journey the 'Fitzjames' brought 430 immigrants, arriving on New Year's Day 1856 and at the time was one of the largest ships to come to South Australia. Tragedy really struck a few years later for on her final journey to Melbourne as an immigrant ship no less than 22 passengers died during the way out from 'ship's fever'.

In the early 1860s, at the conclusion of another Melbourne visit, this time with general cargo only, the condition of the 'Fitzjames' was such that unless major repairs were undertaken she was clearly unfit for the return journey. It was found that those repairs could not be carried out in Melbourne so the owners sold their troublesome ship to a local

The outward appearance of the stylish Largs Pier Hotel has not altered greatly in well over a century.

The gloomy reformatory hulk 'Fitzjames' was moored off Largs throughout the 1880s and it is hard to imagine the feelings of the young lads imprisoned thereon whenever they gazed towards land. The attractive forbidden hotel, then newly built, must have stood out dramatically in the distance and surely the sight of it would have filled them with both wonder and despair. The delinquent and homeless boys on the 'Fitzjames' normally numbered around fifty. During the early years of the hulk's infamous history its youthful prisoners were restricted to only one or two shore visits per year.

business syndicate, who must have envisaged some potential for her in Australian waters.

The 'Fitzjames' turned out to be something of a white elephant for her new owners. For a decade she remained in Hobsons Bay and all the time her condition continued to deteriorate but then came an unexpected and welcome twist of fate. Immigrant ships had been arriving across in South Australia for years carrying cases of smallpox, measles, typhus, scarlatina and other infectious diseases and affected ships were forced to remain offshore for considerable lengths of time. The practice was financially unacceptable to both ship owners and the South Australian Government. A quarantine station was needed. The large, ageing, dismasted 'Fitzjames' was purchased for 2800 pounds and towed to South Australia to provide a temporary solution to the problem. She was to become a quarantine hulk until the time was right for the Government to build a permanent onshore quarantine station.

Authorities might have been well pleased with their purchase but the South Australian public had a few reservations. A newspaper account of the day claimed, 'This was one of their bad bargains. At first sight, with her dingy stumps of masts and her weather-beaten hull she looks as unprepossessing an old ship as ever was taken out of the depths of the sea. It is difficult to say whether the craft is sound in the bottom until she is on the slips.' Another claimed, 'The 'Fitzjames' is the very best picture of a complete wreck. At first, the idea of boarding such a wretched craft was not a comfortable one.'

Well, sound enough the remnants of the 'Fitzjames' must have been for she served as a quarantine hulk for five years, until the establishment of the facilities on Torrens Island.

Now out of service, a little older and perhaps contaminated with who knows what, it was believed the hulk might finally be abandoned. But no, the Destitute Department, who looked after waifs and strays and youthful criminals, bid successfully for the use of the 'Fitzjames'. Their accommodation at Magill and Ilfracombe was overcrowded and the separation and isolation of some of their young male charges could be achieved by housing them offshore. And so began one of the most callous, misguided and horrible actions by our elected leaders.

On March 5th, 1880, thirty-five problem boys were moved in, among them 10-year-old aboriginal Alfred Stokes, who was a world away from his Far North home, and 11-year-old William Edwards from Adelaide. Little Alfred had stolen a watch while William was serving time for being a neglected boy and for 'wandering about'. The sentences of the boys ranged from one to five years and some were aged as young as eight. Their convictions were mainly for stealing or for being uncontrollable but several, like William, were there simply because they were neglected. One little fellow had been placed in custody for 'having dirty habits'.

During the old ship's first few years as a reformatory hulk occasional inspections by members of the press were permitted. All were pre-planned and stage-managed and most subsequent reports tell of smartness and discipline. Dormitories were invariably neat and clean with orderly rows of hammocks and the lads were always busily employed

The imposing Industrial School for destitute children was built at Magill in 1867. Part of it became a boys' reformatory in 1876.

In 1880, the year the above photograph was taken, the boys were transferred to the reformatory hulk 'Fitzjames', moored off Largs Bay. The 'Fitzjames' was previously used as a quarantine hulk and was already in very poor condition. By 1891 the offshore prison was leaking so badly it was finally abandoned and the lads housed once again at Magill.

(Photograph courtesy of East Torrens Historical Society)

stitching clothing, making shoes, working wood or at classes with their slates and books. Everywhere the visitors were taken a uniformed boy would be stationed at the doorway to give them a naval salute. All very impressive.

Then, gradually, reports on the 'Fitzjames' began to delve deeper with questions being asked about the treatment and punishment of the boys, their general living conditions and the unhygienic state of the hulk. In 1883 a Royal Commission headed by Chief Justice Way was established to enquire into the whole working of the Destitute Department and one result of their findings was the transfer of control of the reformatory hulk to the State Childrens' Council.

Revelations were afterwards made public about the punishments handed down regularly for general misbehaviour. It had not been uncommon for a mere boy to be placed on bread and water for up to seven days and whipping was a regular thing. A galvanised iron tub, some old kerosene tins and a ten-gallon keg cut in halves served as lavatories. The boys, who normally numbered around 50, spent very little time on deck and shore visits were restricted to only one or two a year. Little attention was made to correctness of diet and the boys were given no opportunity to exercise. They experienced a depressing, monotonous life.

At the time of the establishment of the reformatory hulk, a stated object of the Destitute Department was that life on board would equip the delinquents with some nautical training, thus preparing them for a life at sea. A few of the lads were actually placed on sailing ships at the conclusion of their sentences but the majority ended up back with their troubled parents or assigned as servants to settlers, always in country districts well away from Adelaide and the town environment.

Many of the inhumanities on the 'Fitzjames' were gradually corrected but others usually took their place. By 1888 the hulk was in extremely poor condition and some timbers were so rotten that the copper sheathing would hardly hold them. She was taking so much water that the lads were continually manning the pumps. They were often at that work, in shifts, from 5.30 a.m. till nightfall. Pressure mounted on the authorities and eventually two men were placed on board to work the pumps. Necessary repairs were commenced although it was generally agreed that whatever work was done would only prolong the inevitable.

The days of the 'Fitzjames' were clearly coming to an end but it was not for another two years, until 1890, that the decision was finally made to move the boys on shore. Delinquent girls were transferred out of the Magill reformatory to new premises at Edwardstown and the 'Fitzjames' boys moved back in.

The almost unrecognisable remnant of the once proud old immigrant ship was towed to the North Arm of the Port River where she was eventually broken up. Nothing now remains to remind us of that dark period of our forefathers' approach to juvenile punishment.

18

Some More Amazing Than Others

Gloucestershire's Forest of Dean was once so famous it was known throughout England as 'the Queen of Forests all'. It was an expanse of unspoilt wilderness where our medieval ancestors frolicked away to their hearts content.

Dark days came however in the 16th century when the forest became the home for scores of gipsy families. Their wandering lifestyle upset the gentle, settled English people and caused considerable hostility, so much so that it became a criminal offence simply to be a gipsy. Several from the Forest of Dean were actually hanged for no other reason, until the laws were thankfully changed in the late 1700s.

But this story is not about race relations and our 'gentle' English ancestors. It concerns another notable feature in the history of 'the Queen of Forests all', its maze, and that maze's connection to South Australia.

In ancient times mazes were quite common. It is believed that their origin goes back to a form of punishment handed out by the Church to wrong-doers. If that is correct, they must have been designed in a really frustrating pattern for today's mazes are nothing more than heaps of fun. One of the most popular designs in medieval England was a number of concentric circles with barriers which blocked some of the paths so formed and openings which led you on or led you nowhere. Generally an open area in the centre awaited the successful. That was the pattern of the Forest of Dean maze.

Our South Australian forebears copied the design when our first maze was established in the Government Farm Reserve at Belair in 1886. There were six circles and hawthorn was selected to create the hedge, the plants being placed about three feet apart. The original plan included a bamboo house within the centre circle but it is not known whether that was ever constructed. The maze's location was within sight of and close access to the Belair Railway Station and it quickly became a popular

The Belair maze was created in 1886 within the Government Farm Reserve, not far from the Belair Railway Station. It quickly became a huge attraction for weekend picnickers who would travel by train from Adelaide.

The Government Farm became Belair National Park in 1891 and the popularity of the maze waned as the centre for broader public activity shifted to the main oval area. In 1902 a second maze was established close to the oval and the original abandoned.

Today the old maze is still discernible. In 1991 major restoration was carried out as part of the National Park's centenary celebrations but there was little follow-up and within a few years, as the above photo shows, the historic recreational attraction was once again overgrown and derelict.

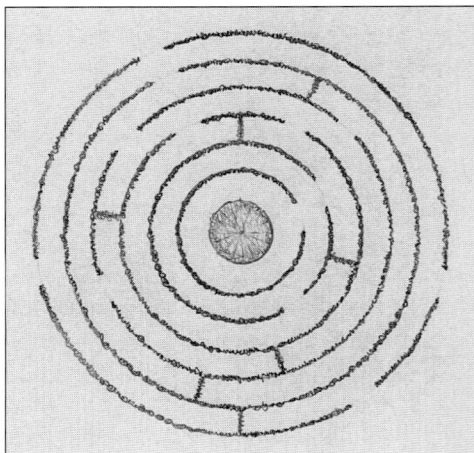

The design of the Belair maze.

venue for weekend parties of picnickers. The area became known as the Belair Recreation Park.

A few years later, in 1891, the Belair National Park was established and that embraced the Recreation Park. In time popularity for the old maze waned and by 1902 it had become overgrown and was rarely used. A replacement was then planted close to the main oval within the National Park, presumably in a more popular area. This second South Australian maze was a direct copy of the first in its design but kaffir apple was used instead of hawthorn. The resulting hedge grew to a height of between four and six feet and was regularly trimmed. Belair maze number two had a much longer life and was finally levelled in 1950, making way for a tennis court.

Restoration of the original maze was commenced in 1988 and completed in 1991 by the South Australian branch of the Australian Garden History Society to part commemorate the National Park's centenary. The project was made possible through a generous National Estate Grant from the Commonwealth Government. The Society's

The Carrick Hill maze is growing nicely but it will be a few years yet before it reaches its desired height. Approximately 2000 box trees were used in its formation.

There are several wooden mazes around South Australia in which maze puzzle lovers can lose themselves. This one is at the Greenhills Adventure Park at Victor Harbor.

splendid work was officially opened towards the end of the year but unfortunately there was little follow-up interest or activity. Within a short time the maze had reverted to its former unkempt, overgrown, derelict condition. Today's remnants of the maze are still worth a visit although reminders of past glories are certainly not such an enjoyable experience as seeing the real thing, or well-kept replicas of the real thing. Let us hope that another longer-lasting rejuvenation of our historic maze will occur one day.

We are fortunate however that we can visit a maze that shows promise and it is not far from the Belair National Park. This delightful hedge-puzzle was planted as recently as 1987, in the vast and beautiful garden of Carrick Hill, that magnificent manorial house at Springfield. Two thousand box trees were used. They are slow growing so it will be a few years yet before the maze reaches its desired height.

There are other mazes in South Australia, including some wooden ones at amusement parks. Like their traditional hedge counterpart at

Carrick Hill, the wooden mazes provide a lot of enjoyment to young and old alike. They can be found at Murray Bridge, Victor Harbor, Monash, St. Kilda and perhaps elsewhere. None however could possibly match the family picnic atmosphere of long ago which surely followed the exciting train trip up into the hills to the Forest of Dean maze in the Belair Recreation Park.

19 *Nullya, Winikeberick, and Pongaree Villa*

On January 10th, 1918, a notice appeared in the South Australian Government Gazette listing no less than 69 names of towns, districts and geographical features around the state that were to be changed. Any name sounding remotely of German origin had to go. Anti-German feeling was at such a pitch throughout World War 1 that the public of South Australia, those of non-German origin, demanded all physical reminders of the arch-enemy of the British Empire be eliminated. The Government responded. The Nomenclature Act of 1917 came into being and Hahndorf, Lobethal and the rest disappeared from the map.

What a headache this turned out to be for the special committee appointed to come up with the names to be changed. German immigrants had been here since shortly after the birth of the colony and had indeed played a major role in the successful development of South Australia. Many of the original families were into their third or even fourth Australian generation by the commencement of the war. They had left their names everywhere – towns, rivers, creeks, hills, rocks, passes, wells, etc. etc. And were all the names that appeared to be German, really German?

One problem for example arose when Mount Schank, that extinct volcano near Mount Gambier, was placed on the list for discussion. Schank certainly sounded German but the mount was actually named after a British Admiral. A descendant of the Admiral, a member of the Conservative Club in London, politely pointed out to the South Australian Government that his was a very ancient English family and that he possessed a family tree going back to the year 1319.

Other problems to be resolved surrounded German names that had been bestowed in recognition of outstanding services by prominent South Australians, such as Dr. Richard Schomburgk, the second Director of the Adelaide Botanic Garden, Mr. F. E. H. Krichauff, at one stage Commissioner of Public Works, Mr. Robert Homburg, an early Attorney-

General and Mr. Alfred von Doussa M.L.C., who had been born in Adelaide and was a major force in opening up land in the Pinnaroo district. Members of the Nomenclature Committee certainly were presented with an awkward task.

None of the above names were retained. The hundred of Schomburgk was re-named Maude, the town of Krichauff became Beatty (which has since been re-named Mount Mary), the hundred of Homburg became Haig and the hundred of von Doussa became Allenby, although Winikeberick had been recommended. A similar case was Ferdinand Creek, in the Musgrave Ranges, named after that wonderful early Australian botanist Ferdinand von Mueller (who has since been memorialised on an Australian postage stamp). Our Parliamentarians of 1917 could not bring themselves to endorse such an 'objectionable' name as Ferdinand and the creek was re-named Ernabella.

Town councils throughout South Australia were also obliged to join in the cull and get rid of all German street names. This meant that some were confronted with wholesale changes. Petersburg, itself to become Peterborough, had a large number of streets bearing

On January 10th, 1918, Hahndorf was one of 69 South Australian German place names Gazetted to be changed. The lovely old Adelaide Hills township was subsequently called Ambleside. Commonsense prevailed in 1935 and its original name was restored.

Ambleside Road is on the outskirts of town but this leads to the site of the original Ambleside, a railway station built about 7km to the north in the early 1880s.

offensive names, such as Bismarck, Glogau, Moltke, Kaiser William, Herman, Koch, Rhode, Rhine. They were mainly replaced with the names of British military leaders of the day and of local men who died during the conflict. It was agreed that the name Petersburg had to go but they fought tooth and nail against the suggested Nullya. That was considered far too insignificant a name, they argued, for such an important town as theirs. The Council eventually won out with their own recommendation, Peterborough. It was generally believed that the town was named after a Mr. Peters, one of the first landholders and shopkeepers of the town.

Many townspeople were of course very unhappy about the changes, particularly those living in the Barossa Valley or the hills towns that had been pioneered by Germans. Lobethal residents objected strongly to the aboriginal Marananga being imposed on them and finally, quite reluctantly, accepted the insipid name of Tweedvale. Marananga was subsequently allotted to Gnadenfrei, near Seppeltsfield, in the Barossa Valley.

Some of the other better known places that were given new identities at the time had their names changed from -

Bethanien to Bethany
Blumburg to Birdwood
Germantown Hill to Vimy Ridge
Hahndorf to Ambleside
Hergott Springs to Maree
Klemzig to Gaza
New Mecklenburg to Gomersal
Rhine River North to the Somme
Rhine River South to the Marne
Rhine Villa to Cambrai
Rosenthal to Rosedale
Steinfeld to Stonefield

These were not always the first choice, many names had been tossed around, recommended then rejected. At one point Hahndorf almost became Yantaringa and Germantown Hill was to be Yarluke Hill, Kombo was chosen for Rosenthal and Pongaree Villa almost won out over Cambrai.

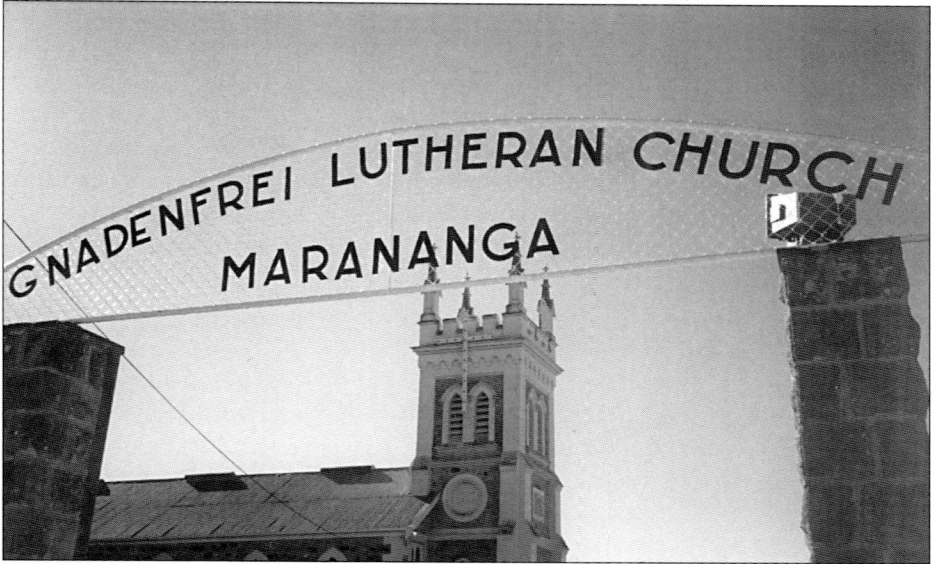

Gnadenfrei, near Seppeltsfield in the Barossa Valley, became Marananga in 1918 when so many South Australian place names of German origin were forced to change.

The district has retained its reluctantly accepted name but the local Lutheran Church makes sure the old name is not forgotten.

The Adelaide Hills township of Lobethal was originally to be called Marananga. The locals objected strongly. They were eventually forced to accept the change but settled instead on the name Tweedvale. Fortunately that old German town is once again known by its original historic name.

Many of the wrongs began being righted in the 1930s and were still being corrected in the 1970s. Lobethal, Klemzig and Hahndorf thankfully have their original names back, as has Germantown Hill but other towns such as Maree, Cambrai and Birdwood retain their revised names.

The Nomenclature Committee had a second duty in 1917, to alter a few names that were duplicated around the state, or that caused confusion to the postal authorities because of similarities. Many of the committee's recommendations were adopted while others were ignored – there is still an Allendale North near Kapunda and there is still an Allendale East down south near Port Macdonnell, despite the proposal to alter the latter to Kandelka – Hilltown missed out on becoming Yakkalo so there is still a Hilltown and a Hilton – there remain two Kingstons, one by Lake Bonney on the Murray River and the other in the south east yet the former did become the town of Thurk from 1918 to 1940. Since then it has been known as Kingston OM, (for 'On Murray') – Yatala in Adelaide's northern suburbs and Yalata on the Eyre Peninsula caused confusion so Yalata became Tarombo before losing its musical name to become Fowler's Bay in 1940 – Tarcowie and Yarcowie resulted in a few headaches so Yarcowie was given the prefix Whyte, in honour of district pioneer John Whyte.

And they had to make decisions on Glencoe and Glencope, a couple of Highburys, Julia and Port Julia, Moorook and Moorak, two Rocky Rivers, Torrens Vale and Torrensville, Calga and Calca, a Franklyn and a Franklin, Geranium and Geranium Plains, the two Lake Bonneys, three Blackfellows Creeks, Port Victor and Port Victoria – the list went on and on, and so did the headaches and arguments.

But back to the German names and the problems for the large number of German descendants living in South Australia. Everyday life became very difficult for them. As well as having to endure the gross insult of their family names being wiped off the map, they were shunned and victimised beyond belief by the righteous South Australians of English backgrounds. One of the less considerate moves by the Government was to close down Lutheran run schools, and there were many of them. No longer would be tolerated such 'insular' education and it was simply too bad for the children if there were no state schools in some of the areas affected.

One can't help wondering what Adelaide might have been re-named had the committee considered the Queen's origins. She was after all the daughter of the Duke of Saxe-Meiningen and her birthplace was well and truly within the boundaries of Germany in 1917. Perhaps the city might have been graciously given Cambrai's reject name, 'Pongaree Villa'. That would have been highly suitable for modern times when the north winds blow over the Bolivar Sewerage Treatment Works.

20 When Hell Broke Loose at Tragedy Dock

Effigies in South Australian graveyards are not very common so when one of a tall fireman is spotted in Cheltenham cemetery you can't help becoming interested. He was meant to draw attention. The beautifully created figure, resplendently crowned in yesteryear's brass helmet, stands head and shoulders above neighbouring angels, columns and crosses.

The inscription on the monument's pedestal reads – "Erected by the citizens of Port Adelaide to the memory of George James Alexandra Anderson and James Hickey, members of the Fire Brigade, who lost their lives in the 'City of Singapore' fire at Port Adelaide, April 26th, 1924".

Another prominent 'fireman memorial' in Adelaide is the Fireman Gardner's drinking fountain in Elder Park. That more familiar monument is interesting because two firemen were killed in the 1886 Rundle Street fire that took Gardner's life. The second, Albert Clark, does not feature on the fountain but is remembered on a more personal basis in North Road cemetery. By a strange coincidence, the Cheltenham memorial is also short on mentioning all who died. Three firefighters, not two, lost their lives in the 'City of Singapore' inferno. The third, also named Albert, was Fireman Greenman.

The 'City of Singapore' was a freighter of about 6500 tons. Its Port Adelaide berth was No. 2 Quay, which lay within a basin known locally as 'Tragedy Dock'. Previous disasters there included the death of a waterside worker when a metal pipe fell on him and a seaman decapitated by a mooring rope that snapped. The name took on new meaning following the terrible events of Saturday evening, 26th April, 1924.

It all started with a small explosion, followed by an isolated fire in No. 4 hold, adjacent to the engine room. The Port Adelaide Fire Brigade was quickly summoned and they in turn called for help from Adelaide's Central Station in Wakefield Street. The 'Fire Queen', Port Adelaide's firefloat, drew alongside and gave assistance as well. After a couple of

No. 2 Quay at Port Adelaide. These days it is often a quiet peaceful haven but on the night of 26th April 1924 it was a scene of nightmarish chaos.

The freighter 'City of Singapore' was berthed here and a fire on board led to explosions that could be seen and heard in the city. Part of the cargo of the large ship were 22,000 cases of motor spirit. Three firemen lost their lives.

Previous disasters nearby included the death of a waterside worker when a metal pipe fell on him and a seaman being decapitated by a mooring rope. The basin became known as 'Tragedy Dock'.

hours and a few small dramas it was thought the fire had been completely extinguished. Then, almost immediately after the 'all-clear' was given, a huge explosion blew out part of the deck and upper works and broke the vessel's back. The explosion was so loud and severe it shook buildings not only at the Port, where a large window of the Town Hall was blown in, but in distant suburbs as well. It was heard for miles. Firemen, policemen and spectators were hurled in all directions, many of them from the ship onto the wharf or into the water. Masses of twisted iron landed amongst spectators and a huge steel ventilator narrowly missed others. Large gaps appeared on the side of the ship. Confusion and panic set in and onlookers ran for their lives.

An inferno began to take over below decks. The fire raged through the stricken vessel and people as far away as the city were treated to an awe-inspiring pyrotechnic display as more and more volatile and explosive material became engulfed. Part of the cargo of the large ship were 22,000 cases of motor spirit for the Vacuum Oil Company.

The steamer was quite new, having been launched the previous year, 1923. She had arrived at Port Adelaide from New York via the eastern Australian ports and at the time of the fire was discharging the motor spirit along with motor cars and other American goods. At the same time, wheat and flour were being loaded, destined for South Africa. About 600 tons of wheat had already been lowered into one of the six holds before the fire started.

There were many casualties. Fireman Albert Greenman was killed outright, his body being found further down the wharf. Anderson and Hickey remained unaccounted for and their bodies were never recovered. At least a dozen other firefighters were in a serious condition with burns, broken limbs, cuts and abrasions and shock. Ambulances and private cars quickly conveyed those injured to the Port Adelaide Casualty Hospital, next door to the Town Hall.

The masses who assembled at the scene witnessed many acts of heroism in the ensuing attempts to rescue trapped and injured seamen and

This tall effigy of a fireman stands head and shoulders above neighbouring angels, columns and crosses in the Cheltenham cemetery. The eye-catching memorial commemorates two of the three firemen who died in the calamitous 1924 fire on the freighter 'City of Singapore'.

101

firefighters. It was believed that large quantities of the motor spirit remained in the holds and further explosions could occur at any time. Men were however trapped and caution was thrown to the wind by a very special group consisting of a policeman, three civilians and the ship's Chief Officer. Together they descended into various quarters of the blazing ship where it was felt someone might still be alive. At one stage a faint cry was heard from lower down in the stokehold and two of the men managed to get to and rescue an engineer who would have been doomed to a nightmarish death. In doing so they had to find their way along a number of passages and wriggle their way through a small aperture with their only means of visibility being the light from their torches and from the surrounding fire. The engineer's only way of escape from his hell-hole, the ladder, had been destroyed. Chief Officer Jeffries actually lowered himself into the hold by a rope and literally snatched the panic-stricken man from the flames – an almost unbelievable act of bravery. It was revealed later that Jeffries had been injured himself during the early stages of the fire, had been treated at the Casualty Hospital and returned with a bandaged head to become involved in the rescue mission.

Fireman Albert Greenman was attached to the Central Fire Station in Wakefield Street and lived with his wife and mother in a house at the rear of the station. Fireman James Hickey, who came to Adelaide from Coonawarra, was also attached to Wakefield Street and was single. Fireman Anderson was a member of the Port Adelaide Brigade and was a member of the Naval Reserve.

The imposing statue of the single fireman in the Cheltenham cemetery stands as a memorial not just to the two mentioned on its pedestal but to many men touched by that calamitous Saturday night at Port Adelaide.

The 'City of Singapore' was practically a new ship on her arrival at Port Adelaide but appeared to be a total wreck following the explosion. Overseas salvage expert W. J. Russell bought the steamer from the underwriters and arranged for it to be towed all the way to Rotterdam, in Holland. At the time it became the world's record tow, a distance of 13,000 miles over almost five months. She was in tow of two powerful Dutch tug boats. The stricken steamer was subsequently fully repaired and repurchased by her original owners.

21

A Memorial Here, A Memorial There, A Memorial Just About Everywhere

Charles Sturt lived in South Australia for just 14 years, from 1839 to 1853, yet considerably more memorials have been erected or unveiled here in his honour than similar memorials for any other South Australian. Add to that the incredible number of place names and geographical features that bear his name and one realizes how special a man Sturt must have been.

Let's face it, who else could possibly have been memorialised in brass and stone around 20 times and also have named after him a highway, several streets, roads and lanes, two suburbs, a river, a county, a bay, a point, a mountain, a valley, a desert – not to mention the state's floral emblem, a paddlesteamer, a football club, numerous pubs, etc., etc. The list goes on, right down to a section within Adelaide's West Terrace Cemetery, to nursing homes and pizza bars. And that's only in South Australia for Sturt is equally remembered in New South Wales and Victoria.

There is no doubt that Charles Sturt was a great explorer. It is well recorded that results from his two heroic expeditions, down the Murray in 1830 and into Central Australia in 1844, added immensely to known facts about Australia at the time and greatly influenced follow-up decision making. There were however other explorers who achieved equally as much so why the huge imbalance in the number of memorials?

It would seem that Sturt's exploits really captured the imagination of the people. He became something of a romantic figure in Australian folklore. This was very evident around 1930, the centenary year of his mighty river journey, when the Sturt Centenary Expedition was planned and carried out by the Royal Geographical Society of New South Wales and the Historical Memorials Committees of Victoria and New South Wales. A party of dignitaries journeyed from one river town to the next,

Almost hidden by the long riverside grass is the memorial to Sturt at Kingston. The plaque is missing. It carried the fascinating inscription, 'Near this spot, Capt. Sturt, pioneer explorer, had an exciting experience with natives in January 1830'.

Some of the many memorials to Charles Sturt indicate how it must have been assumed at the time that everyone knew exactly who he was. This one is at Wellington.

CAPT. CHARLES STURT

PASSED HERE ON

9TH. FEBRUARY 1830

Charles Sturt is remembered in South Australia through approximately 20 memorials, a highway, several streets, roads and lanes, two suburbs, a river, a county, a bay, a point, a mountain, a valley, a desert – not to mention the state's floral emblem, a paddlesteamer, a football club, numerous pubs, etc. etc. The list goes on, right down to a section within Adelaide's West Terrace cemetery, to nursing homes and pizza bars.

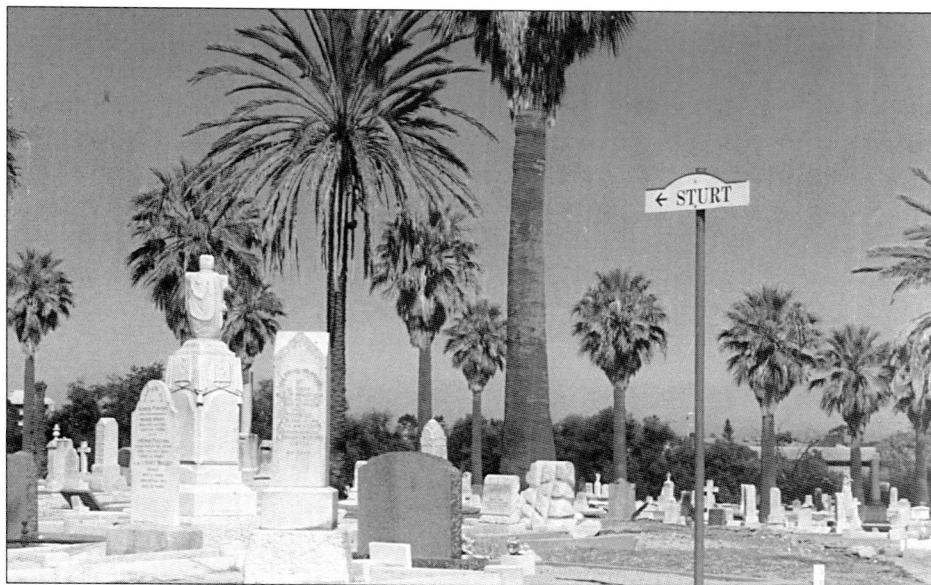

making lengthy, glowing speeches about Sturt's achievements of one hundred years before and at each stopover unveiled a memorial.

The first ceremony held in South Australia was at Renmark and the final on Hindmarsh Island, at a point not far from the Murray mouth where the 1830 river journey ended. On the way, memorials were unveiled at Loxton, Kingston, Morgan, Mannum, Milang and Point McLeay. Locals took the opportunity to recognise other pioneers at the same time for the party also participated in unveiling the Chaffey memorial at Renmark and the Ernest Loveday drinking fountain at Loveday. Similarly, on the Hindmarsh Island cairn Captain Collet Barker was honoured along with Sturt.

Three more South Australian river towns were added at a later date to those with Sturt memorials – Wellington, Berri and Barmera. The feeling towards Sturt in the 1930s and the then belief that simply everyone was familiar with his story can be gauged from the wording on a couple of the plaques. All we read at Wellington is, "Capt. Charles Sturt passed here on 9th February 1830", while at Milang there is not much more, "Captain Charles Sturt passed this place February 1830, erected 1930." Clearly there was no need to tell passers-by who Captain Sturt was for everyone knew.

Most of the string of memorials are still in good condition but unfortunately the most interesting of all has lost its brass plaque. The Kingston cairn once carried the story, "Near this spot, Capt. Sturt, pioneer explorer, had an exciting experience with natives in January 1830". During the speeches at the 1930 ceremony it was stated, "It was built near a highway where it would be permanently brought under the notice of every man, woman and child." Perhaps that was its undoing.

The "exciting experience" referred to was the incident that could very well have ended the expedition. The party was threatened by a large number of spear-brandishing natives but any actual encounter was thwarted by the intervention of a man befriended by Sturt some days earlier.

The Barmera memorial is a little different to the others. It is the clock tower in the middle of the main street. It also commemorates a different expedition to those in the other river towns for it remembers Sturt's 1844 visit to the area, when he surveyed and camped by Lake Bonney shortly after the commencement of his trek to Central Australia.

At least four other Sturt memorials exist to remind us of the 1844 expedition. Two are in the city, one is at Gawler and the other is at

Koonunga, where Sturt rested at the home of pioneer pastoralist Charles Hervey Bagot. One of those in the city is Sturt's statue in Victoria Square. He stands there with one hand shading his eyes as he stares far into the distance, forever looking for that elusive inland sea, one of the prime objects of his and of others' explorations.

There is, or was, yet another memorial, a very different one that was possibly left by Sturt himself.

Up river from Renmark a very old, very large river gum stood majestically overlooking the Murray. It carried the scar of a 9-meter native canoe which had been cut from it in the distant past. It also carried another scar, the inscription "SME 20". Local legend tells us that the carving was possibly made by a member of Sturt's party when they camped beside the tree on their 1830 river voyage of discovery. It was suggested that "SME 20" signified Sturt's Murray Expedition, 20th campsite.

The 'SME 20' inscribed on this 700 to 1000-year-old river gum upstream from Renmark was believed to have been carved by a member of Sturt's 1830 Murray expedition, the '20' referring to their 20th campsite. A huge Aboriginal bark canoe had been cut from the reverse side in distant times.

As recent as 1996 that wonderful 700 to 1000-year-old icon was destroyed by fire left by careless holiday-makers. What a frightful loss to both the traditional owners of the land and to all South Australians. Fortunately stone cairns can be repaired and brass plaques replaced so, unlike the tree, the many official memorials around the state will continue to remind present and future generations of the wonderful achievements of Captain Charles Sturt.

The Sturt/canoe tree was sadly destroyed by fire left by careless campers in 1996.

About the Author

RUSSELL SMITH has had a wide mixture of writings published – a book through Shakespeare Head Press, "1850, A VERY GOOD YEAR IN THE COLONY OF SOUTH AUSTRALIA" – a story in the Bicentennial Authority book, "UNSUNG HEROES & HEROINES OF AUSTRALIA" – the winning play in the playwriting competition held for South Australia's 150th, "THE BATTLE OF VINEGAR HILL" , which was subsequently produced at the Arts Theatre – a long-running series of bush verse and photos in Australasian Post entitled, "TALES FROM TANKAROOKA" – South Australian based crosswords compiled for "COMMUNITY HISTORY", the magazine of the History Trust of South Australia – articles and crosswords for "STATEWIDE" newspaper – other history-based articles in various magazines and newspapers – and in 1998, "CURIOSITIES OF SOUTH AUSTRALIA". Number 2 in this series now follows.

Russell works in semi-retirement as an attendant at the Bicentennial Conservatory in Adelaide's Botanic Garden and at every opportunity, with wife Pam, is off somewhere around the state taking photographs and searching out more interesting and unusual stories. Pam then spends a good deal of her time with follow-up research and generally assisting with the preparation of the stories.